most loved recipe collection most loved recipe collection most loved recipe collection most loved recipe collection most loved recipe collection most loved recipe collection most loved recipe collection most loved recipe collection most loved recipe collection most loved recipe collection most loved recipe collection most loved recipe collection most loved recipe collection most loved recipe collection most loved recipe collection most loved recipe collection most loved recipe collection most loved recipe collection

most loved

Slow Cooker
creations

Pictured on front cover:
Pot Roast, page 46

Pictured on back cover:
Coq Au Vin, page 72

Most Loved Slow Cooker Creations
Copyright © Company's Coming Publishing Limited

All rights reserved worldwide. No part of this book may be reproduced, stored in a retrieval system or transmitted in any form by any means without written permission in advance from the publisher.

In the case of photocopying or other reprographic copying, a license may be purchased from the Canadian Copyright Licensing Agency (Access Copyright). Visit www.accesscopyright.ca or call toll free 1-800-893-5777. In the United States, please contact the Copyright Clearance Centre at www.copyright.com or call 978-646-8600.

Brief portions of this book may be reproduced for review purposes, provided credit is given to the source. Reviewers are invited to contact the publisher for additional information.

Second Printing February 2009

Library and Archives Canada Cataloguing in Publication
Paré, Jean, date
Most loved slow cooker creations / Jean Paré.
(Most loved recipe collection)
Includes index.
ISBN 978-1-897069-18-9
1. Electric cookery, Slow. I. Title. II. Series: Paré, Jean, date-
Most loved recipe collection.
TX827.P3685 2008   641.5'884   C2007-903677-5

Published by
Company's Coming Publishing Limited
2311 – 96 Street
Edmonton, Alberta, Canada T6N 1G3
Tel: 780-450-6223   Fax: 780-450-1857
www.companyscoming.com

Company's Coming is a registered trademark owned by Company's Coming Publishing Limited

We acknowledge the financial support of the Government of Canada through the Book Publishing Industry Development Program (BPIDP) for our publishing activities.

Printed in China

We gratefully acknowledge the following suppliers for their generous support of our Test and Photography Kitchens:

Broil King Barbecues
Corelle®
Hamilton Beach® Canada
Lagostina®
Proctor Silex® Canada
Tupperware®

Our special thanks to the following businesses for providing props for photography:

Casa Bugatti
Cherison Enterprises Inc.
Chintz & Company
Creations By Design
Danesco Inc.
Emile Henry
Hamilton Beach® Canada
Le Gnome
Linens 'N Things
Mikasa Home Store
Out of the Fire Studio
Pier 1 Imports
Pfaltzgraff Canada
Pyrex®
Scona Clayworks
Stokes
The Basket House
The Bay
Totally Bamboo
Treasure Barrel
Winners Stores
Zenari's

Pictured from left: Slow Cooker Dolmades, page 34; Chicken And Dumpling Soup, page 30; Cajun Chicken, page 76; Hot Tea Wassail, page 8.

table of contents

the Company's Coming story

"never share a recipe you wouldn't use yourself"

Jean Paré (pronounced "jeen PAIR-ee") grew up understanding that the combination of family, friends and home cooking is the best recipe for a good life. From her mother, she learned to appreciate good cooking, while her father praised even her earliest attempts in the kitchen. When Jean left home, she took with her a love of cooking, many family recipes and an intriguing desire to read cookbooks as if they were novels!

When her four children had all reached school age, Jean volunteered to cater the 50th anniversary celebration of the Vermilion School of Agriculture, now Lakeland College, in Alberta, Canada. Working out of her home, Jean prepared a dinner for more than 1,000 people, launching a flourishing catering operation that continued for over 18 years. During that time, she had countless opportunities to test new ideas with immediate feedback—resulting in empty plates and contented customers! Whether preparing cocktail sandwiches for a house party or serving a hot meal for 1,500 people, Jean Paré earned a reputation for great food, courteous service and reasonable prices.

As requests for her recipes increased, Jean was often asked the question, "Why don't you write a cookbook?" Jean responded by teaming up with her son, Grant Lovig, in the fall of 1980 to form Company's Coming Publishing Limited. The publication of 150 Delicious Squares on April 14, 1981 marked the debut of what would soon become one of the world's most popular cookbook series.

The company has grown since those early days when Jean worked from a spare bedroom in her home. Today, she continues to write recipes while working closely with the staff of the Recipe Factory, as the Company's Coming test kitchen is affectionately known. There she fills the role of mentor, assisting with the development of recipes people most want to use for everyday cooking and easy entertaining. Every Company's Coming recipe is kitchen-tested before it is approved for publication.

Jean's daughter, Gail Lovig, is responsible for marketing and distribution, leading a team that includes sales personnel located in major cities across Canada. Company's Coming cookbooks are distributed in Canada, the United States, Australia and other world markets. Bestsellers many times over in English, Company's Coming cookbooks have also been published in French and Spanish.

Familiar and trusted in home kitchens around the world, Company's Coming cookbooks are offered in a variety of formats. Highly regarded as kitchen workbooks, the softcover Original Series, with its lay-flat plastic comb binding, is still a favourite among readers.

Jean Paré's approach to cooking has always called for quick and easy recipes using everyday ingredients. That view has served her well. The recipient of many awards, including the Queen Elizabeth Golden Jubilee Medal, Jean was appointed Member of the Order of Canada, her country's highest lifetime achievement honour.

Jean continues to gain new supporters by adhering to what she calls The Golden Rule of Cooking: Never share a recipe you wouldn't use yourself. It's an approach that has worked—millions of times over!

foreword

For a while in the '70s and '80s, it seemed that almost every bride had to write a thank-you note for a slow cooker. Often she used it once or twice, and then relegated it to the back of a kitchen cupboard with her husband's college drinking mugs. In the 1990s, the slow cooker would show up again, but at flea markets or garage sales.

So why is there such a slow cooker revival in the new millennium? To begin with, manufacturers have updated the rather dowdy look of the original models, creating sleek, stainless steel versions that look fabulous on any counter.

More importantly, we're all beginning to realize that a fast food diet isn't doing us, or our families, much good. But how can we get a healthy, homemade meal on the table when our busy lives have us spending time everywhere but in our kitchens? A slow cooker can gently simmer away all day, and the only thing you have to do is get home in time to enjoy it. You control the fat, the salt and every other ingredient in your family's meal.

With *Most Loved Slow Cooker Creations*, a treasury of favourite recipes published over the years at Company's Coming, we show you how to serve up great-tasting entrees such as Coq Au Vin, Corned Beef Brisket and Barbecued Shredded Pork Sandwiches. Our Slow Cooker Dolmades are always a hit (and a great potluck dish), while our wonderful party beverages let you take part in the fun without having to fuss over drinks. And if all you want is a steaming bowl of something filling when you come in on a winter evening, check out our Tex-Mex Taco Soup or our hot-and-sour Chinese Mushroom Soup.

All you need to do is pop the ingredients into your slow cooker before you go out the door. If mornings are too hectic, do your slicing and dicing the night before (preferably while the rest of the family is doing the dishes!). Fill the slow cooker, pop the liner in the fridge and stick it into your slow cooker before you leave for the day. You can spend the day anticipating the delicious meal you'll enjoy when you get home that night!

Jean Paré

nutrition information

Each recipe is analyzed using the most current version of the Canadian Nutrient File from Health Canada, which is based on the United States Department of Agriculture (USDA) Nutrient Database.

- If more than one ingredient is listed (such as "butter or hard margarine"), or if a range is given (1 – 2 tsp., 5 – 10 mL), only the first ingredient or first amount is analyzed.

- For meat, poultry and fish, the serving size per person is based on the recommended 4 oz. (113 g) uncooked weight (without bone), which is 2 – 3 oz. (57 – 85 g) cooked weight (without bone)—approximately the size of a deck of playing cards.

- Milk used is 1% M.F. (milk fat), unless otherwise stated.

- Cooking oil used is canola oil, unless otherwise stated.

- Ingredients indicating "sprinkle," "optional," or "for garnish" are not included in the nutrition information.

- The fat in recipes and combination foods can vary greatly depending on the sources and types of fats used in each specific ingredient. For these reasons, the amount of saturated, monounsaturated and polyunsaturated fats may not add up to the total fat content.

Vera C. Mazurak, Ph.D.
Nutritionist

The spicy apple aroma of this hot toddy will fill your house with a festive scent. Garnish each mug with a fresh cinnamon stick for a little added flair. Cut out the brandy to make it kid-friendly.

Cranberry Apple Warmer

Apple juice	4 cups	1 L
Cranberry cocktail	4 cups	1 L
Water	2 cups	500 mL
Brown sugar, packed	1/4 cup	60 mL
Cinnamon sticks (4 inches, 10 cm, each)	3	3
Ground nutmeg	1/4 tsp.	1 mL
Brandy (optional)	1/2 cup	125 mL

Combine first 6 ingredients in 3 1/2 to 4 quart (3.5 to 4 L) slow cooker. Cook, covered, on Low for 6 to 7 hours or on High for 3 to 3 1/2 hours. Discard cinnamon sticks. Makes about 10 cups (2.5 L).

Divide brandy into 8 mugs. Add cranberry mixture. Stir. Serves 8.

1 serving: 153 Calories; 0.2 g Total Fat (trace Mono, 0.1 g Poly, trace Sat); 0 mg Cholesterol; 39 g Carbohydrate; 0 g Fibre; 0 g Protein; 10 mg Sodium

Pictured at right.

Life is short—eat dessert first! Dress up this rich and creamy treat with a dash of your favourite nut-flavoured liqueur.

Caramel Hot Chocolate

Water	6 cups	1.5 L
Skim milk powder	2 cups	500 mL
Can of sweetened condensed milk	11 oz.	300 mL
Cocoa, sifted if lumpy	3/4 cup	175 mL
Caramel flavouring syrup	1/2 cup	125 mL

Miniature multi-coloured marshmallows,
   for garnish

Combine first 4 ingredients in 3 1/2 to 4 quart (3.5 to 4 L) slow cooker. Cook, covered, on Low for about 6 hours or on High for about 3 hours until boiling.

Add syrup. Stir until smooth.

Garnish individual servings with marshmallows. Makes about 8 cups (2 L).

1 cup (250 mL): 301 Calories; 4.7 g Total Fat (0.4 g Mono, 0.2 g Poly, 2.9 g Sat); 19 mg Cholesterol; 53 g Carbohydrate; 2 g Fibre; 16 g Protein; 264 mg Sodium

Pictured at right.

1. Cranberry Apple Warmer, page 6
2. Caramel Hot Chocolate, page 6
3. Hot Buttered Cranberry, page 10

With the warming qualities of tea, mulled wine and apple cider, wassail (pronounced WAHS-uhl) is the ultimate winter warmer-upper. Brew up this bevvie whenever the mercury heads south.

about slow cooker sizes

Slow cookers come in a variety of sizes from the very wee, used to make dips and fondues, to the quite mammoth, used to feed larger numbers. Generally, the most popular sizes range from 3.5 to 5 quarts (3.5 to 5 L). When choosing a slow cooker, don't just opt for a larger size and assume it will work well with small quantities. In order to cook evenly and in the time stated in the recipe, a slow cooker must be filled at least half full—unless stated otherwise. So always use the size suggested in the recipe.

Hot Tea Wassail

Boiling water	6 cups	1.5 L
Orange pekoe tea bags	4	4
Dry (or alcohol-free) red wine	3 cups	750 mL
Large lemon, cut into 1/2 inch (12 mm) thick slices	1	1
Liquid honey	1/2 cup	125 mL
Cinnamon sticks (4 inches, 10 cm, each)	2	2
Small unpeeled cooking apples (such as McIntosh), cored	3	3
Whole allspice	12	12
Whole cloves	12	12

Pour boiling water over tea bags in 3 1/2 to 4 quart (3.5 to 4 L) slow cooker. Let steep, covered, for 10 minutes. Squeeze and discard tea bags.

Add next 4 ingredients. Stir.

Pierce skin on apples several times with tip of paring knife. Push allspice and cloves into slits in apples. Add to wine mixture. Cook, covered, on Low for 2 hours. Strain and discard solids. Makes about 10 cups (2.5 L).

1 cup (250 mL): 115 Calories; 0 g Total Fat (0 g Mono, 0 g Poly, 0 g Sat); 0 mg Cholesterol; 15 g Carbohydrate; 0 g Fibre; trace Protein; 3 mg Sodium

Pictured at right.

The relatively small amount of butter in this spiced cranberry drink adds a richness and body you don't traditionally find in mulled drinks. Excellent!

hot spiced cranberry

You can lighten up a bit and omit the butter—it still makes a great sweet treat.

Hot Buttered Cranberry

Pineapple juice	4 cups	1 L
Cans of jellied cranberry sauce (14 oz., 398 mL, each)	2	2
Water	3 cups	750 mL
Brown sugar, packed	1/2 cup	125 mL
Ground cinnamon	1/2 tsp.	2 mL
Ground cloves	1/2 tsp.	2 mL
Ground allspice	1/4 tsp.	1 mL
Ground nutmeg	1/4 tsp.	1 mL
Salt	1/8 tsp.	0.5 mL
Butter	1/4 cup	60 mL
Dark (navy) rum (optional)	1 cup	250 mL

Combine first 9 ingredients in 3 1/2 to 4 quart (3.5 to 4 L) slow cooker. Cook, covered, on Low for 4 hours.

Add butter and rum. Stir until butter is melted. Makes about 12 cups (3 L).

1 cup (250 mL): 212 Calories; 3.9 g Total Fat (1.0 g Mono, 0.2 g Poly, 2.4 g Sat); 10 mg Cholesterol; 46 g Carbohydrate; 1 g Fibre; trace Protein; 76 mg Sodium

Pictured on page 7.

Dress up your regular red wine in grand style by adding citrus juice and spices—the result will be a sweet departure from the everyday. Garnish with fresh orange slices.

cranberry mulled wine

For a more tart treat, use the same amount of cranberry cocktail instead of orange juice.

Mulled Wine

Dry (or alcohol-free) red wine	8 cups	2 L
Orange juice	2 cups	500 mL
Corn syrup	2/3 cup	150 mL
Medium unpeeled orange, sliced	1	1
Lemon juice	1 tsp.	5 mL
Cinnamon sticks (4 inches, 10 cm, each), broken up and crushed	3	3
Whole allspice	1 tsp.	5 mL
Whole cloves	1 tsp.	5 mL

Combine first 5 ingredients in 3 1/2 to 4 quart (3.5 to 4 L) slow cooker.

(continued on next page)

Place next 3 ingredients on 10 inch (25 cm) square of double-layered cheesecloth. Draw up corners and tie with string. Submerge in liquid in slow cooker. Cook, covered, on Low for 3 hours. Remove and discard spice bag. Discard orange slices. Makes about 9 cups (2.25 L).

1 cup (250 mL): 271 Calories; 0.2 g Total Fat (trace Mono, trace Poly, trace Sat); 0 mg Cholesterol; 30 g Carbohydrate; 0 g Fibre; 1 g Protein; 46 mg Sodium

Pictured below.   Mulled Wine, page 10

For those who think the spice is right, this hot-and-sour soup full of crunchy bamboo and water chestnuts is sure to heat things up—and the addition of chewy Chinese mushrooms makes this brothy best a filling meal.

variation

Have some leftovers in your fridge? Use the same amount of diced cooked beef, chicken, shrimp or tofu instead of pork.

Chinese Mushroom Soup

Chinese dried mushrooms	15	15
Boiling water	2 cups	500 mL
Prepared chicken broth	6 cups	1.5 L
Can of shoestring-style bamboo shoots, drained	8 oz.	227 mL
Can of sliced water chestnuts, drained	8 oz.	227 mL
Rice vinegar	1/3 cup	75 mL
Soy sauce	1/4 cup	60 mL
Dried crushed chilies	1 tsp.	5 mL
Diced cooked pork	1 cup	250 mL
Sliced green onion	2 tbsp.	30 mL

Put mushrooms into small heatproof bowl. Add boiling water. Stir. Let stand for about 20 minutes until softened. Drain. Remove and discard stems. Slice thinly. Transfer to 3 1/2 to 4 quart (3.5 to 4 L) slow cooker.

Add next 6 ingredients. Stir. Cook, covered, on Low for 8 to 10 hours or on High for 4 to 5 hours.

Add pork and green onion. Stir well. Cook, covered, on High for 10 to 15 minutes until heated through. Makes about 8 1/2 cups (2.1 L).

1 cup (250 mL): 117 Calories; 4.7 g Total Fat (2.0 g Mono, 0.6 g Poly, 1.6 g Sat); 14 mg Cholesterol; 10 g Carbohydrate; 3 g Fibre; 9 g Protein; 936 mg Sodium

Pictured at right.

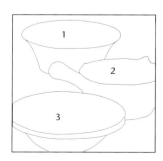

1. Scotch Broth, page 15
2. French Onion Soup, page 14
3. Chinese Mushroom Soup, above

This rich and hearty, chock-full-of-goodness soup is packed to the brim with beef and veggies. It makes the perfect wintry evening supper when served with garlic bread or crusty rolls.

Beef Vegetable Soup

Cooking oil	2 tsp.	10 mL
Lean ground beef	1 lb.	454 g
Water	3 cups	750 mL
Can of diced tomatoes (with juice)	14 oz.	398 mL
Diced peeled potato	1 1/2 cups	375 mL
Frozen mixed vegetables	1 1/2 cups	375 mL
Can of condensed tomato soup	10 oz.	284 mL
Chopped onion	1 cup	250 mL
Thinly sliced carrot	1 cup	250 mL
Diced celery	1/2 cup	125 mL
Granulated sugar	1 tsp.	5 mL
Salt	1/2 tsp.	2 mL
Pepper	1/4 tsp.	1 mL
Liquid gravy browner (optional)	1 tsp.	5 mL

Heat cooking oil in large frying pan on medium. Add beef. Scramble-fry for about 10 minutes until no longer pink. Drain. Transfer to 4 to 5 quart (4 to 5 L) slow cooker.

Add remaining 12 ingredients. Stir. Cook, covered, on Low for 9 to 10 hours or on High for 4 1/2 to 5 hours. Makes about 11 cups (2.75 L).

1 cup (250 mL): 147 Calories; 4.6 g Total Fat (1.9 g Mono, 0.7 g Poly, 1.5 g Sat); 23 mg Cholesterol; 17 g Carbohydrate; 3 g Fibre; 11 g Protein; 403 mg Sodium

You can get just as fancy as you please with your slow cooker—and this decadent soup is case in point. Topped with the traditional cheese-laden croûte (toasted bread slice), this recipe is proof that fine dining is just a slow cooker away.

French Onion Soup

Thinly sliced onion	4 cups	1 L
Water	4 cups	1 L
Beef bouillon powder	4 tsp.	20 mL
French bread slices (1/4 inch, 6 mm, thick)	8	8
Grated mozzarella cheese	1 cup	250 mL
Grated Parmesan cheese, sprinkle		

Combine first 3 ingredients in 3 1/2 to 4 quart (3.5 to 4 L) slow cooker. Cook, covered, on Low for 8 to 10 hours or on High for 4 to 5 hours. Makes about 5 1/2 cups (1.4 L).

(continued on next page)

Ladle soup into 4 ovenproof bowls. Place on baking sheet with sides. Place 2 bread slices over soup in each bowl. Sprinkle 1/4 cup (60 mL) mozzarella cheese over each. Sprinkle with Parmesan cheese. Broil on centre rack in oven until cheese is bubbly and golden. Serves 4.

1 serving: 257 Calories; 8.0 g Total Fat (2.6 g Mono, 0.6 g Poly, 4.3 g Sat); 24 mg Cholesterol; 36 g Carbohydrate; 3 g Fibre; 11 g Protein; 1134 mg Sodium

Pictured on page 13.

Scotch Broth

Cooking oil	1 tbsp.	15 mL
Stewing lamb (or beef), trimmed of fat and cut into 1/2 inch (12 mm) pieces	1 1/2 lbs.	680 g
Prepared beef broth	8 cups	2 L
Chopped onion	2 cups	500 mL
Chopped carrot	1 1/2 cups	375 mL
Chopped yellow turnip	1 cup	250 mL
Pearl barley	2/3 cup	150 mL
Chopped celery	1/2 cup	125 mL
Salt	1/8 tsp.	0.5 mL
Pepper	1/4 tsp.	1 mL
Frozen peas	1/2 cup	125 mL
Chopped fresh parsley (or 1 tbsp., 15 mL, flakes)	1/4 cup	60 mL

Kick up yer kilts! This unique soup made with lamb and barley is sure to put some hop in your Scotch.

Heat cooking oil in large frying pan on medium-high. Add lamb. Cook for 8 to 10 minutes, stirring occasionally, until browned. Transfer to 4 to 5 quart (4 to 5 L) slow cooker.

Add next 8 ingredients. Stir. Cook, covered, on Low for 8 to 10 hours or on High for 4 to 5 hours.

Add peas and parsley. Stir. Cook, covered, on High for about 5 minutes until peas are tender. Makes about 12 cups (3 L).

1 cup (250 mL): 174 Calories; 4.7 g Total Fat (1.9 g Mono, 0.7 g Poly, 1.2 g Sat); 37 mg Cholesterol; 19 g Carbohydrate; 3 g Fibre; 14 g Protein; 405 mg Sodium

Pictured on page 13.

Don't tie yourself to the stove—this Thai delight is made in your slow cooker. Creamy carrots, peanut undertones and a gentle spicy heat make this soup vibrant and velvety.

Carrot Satay Soup

Prepared chicken broth	3 cups	750 mL
Sliced carrot	3 cups	750 mL
Chopped onion	1 cup	250 mL
Chopped celery	1/2 cup	125 mL
Brown sugar, packed	2 tbsp.	30 mL
Finely grated gingerroot	2 tsp.	10 mL
(or 1/2 tsp., 2 mL, ground ginger)		
Garlic cloves, minced	2	2
(or 1/2 tsp., 2 mL, powder)		
Salt	1/4 tsp.	1 mL
Cayenne pepper	1/8 tsp.	0.5 mL
Cream cheese, softened	1/4 cup	60 mL
Smooth peanut butter	3 tbsp.	50 mL
Soy sauce	1 tbsp.	15 mL
Sesame seeds, toasted (see Tip), for garnish		

Combine first 9 ingredients in 3 1/2 to 4 quart (3.5 to 4 L) slow cooker. Cook, covered, on Low for 5 to 6 hours or on High for 2 1/2 to 3 hours.

Add next 3 ingredients. Stir. Carefully process with hand blender or in blender until smooth (see Safety Tip).

Garnish individual servings with sesame seeds. Makes about 6 cups (1.5 L).

1 cup (250 mL): 152 Calories; 8.2 g Total Fat (2.2 g Mono, 1.4 g Poly, 3.3 g Sat); 10 mg Cholesterol; 17 g Carbohydrate; 3 g Fibre; 5 g Protein; 1060 mg Sodium

Pictured at right.

Safety Tip: Follow manufacturer's instructions for processing hot liquids.

Left: Curried Cauliflower Soup, page 21
Right: Carrot Satay Soup, above

No need to man the helm—your slow cooker will take over in our version of this traditional tomato-based clam chowder. Serve with buns or crusty bread for dunking.

Manhattan Clam Chowder

Cans of whole baby clams (5 oz., 142 g, each)	2	2
Water	6 cups	1.5 L
Cans of diced tomatoes (with juice), 14 oz. (398 mL) each	2	2
Chopped onion	2 cups	500 mL
Chopped unpeeled red potato	2 cups	500 mL
Diced celery	1 cup	250 mL
Can of tomato paste	5 1/2 oz.	156 mL
Diced carrot	1/2 cup	125 mL
Bacon slices, cooked crisp and crumbled	5	5
Dried thyme	1 tsp.	5 mL
Cayenne pepper	1/4 tsp.	1 mL

Drain liquid from clams into 5 to 7 quart (5 to 7 L) slow cooker. Transfer clams to small bowl. Chill, covered.

Add next 10 ingredients to slow cooker. Stir. Cook, covered, on Low for 8 to 10 hours or on High for 4 to 5 hours. Add clams. Stir. Cook, covered, on High for about 10 minutes until heated through. Makes about 14 cups (3.5 L).

1 cup (250 mL): 88 Calories; 1.7 g Total Fat (0.4 g Mono, 0.2 g Poly, 0.5 g Sat); 19 mg Cholesterol; 14 g Carbohydrate; 2 g Fibre; 6 g Protein; 335 mg Sodium

Pictured at right.

Top: Manhattan Clam Chowder, above
Bottom: Chunky Zucchini Soup, page 20

Loaded with veggies and the fine flavours of smoky ham and dill, this unique soup is the perfect fare to bring to your next potluck—and your slow cooker is the perfect carrying case!

food fun

Dill has been a household staple for years—since 400 B.C., some historians assert. And although we know and love dill as a food additive, it seems our ancestors used it for almost everything but. Dill seeds were burned in the home as an all-natural air freshener. Dill tea was given to people who had trouble sleeping, and medicinally it was used to settle all sorts of tummy troubles. But perhaps the most paradoxical use of dill concerned witches. Dill was suggested to repel witches, yet witches were also reported to favour it in their potion-making.

Chunky Zucchini Soup

Chopped zucchini (with peel)	4 cups	1 L
Chopped peeled potato	3 cups	750 mL
All-purpose flour	1/4 cup	60 mL
Prepared chicken broth	6 cups	1.5 L
Sliced leek (white part only)	3 cups	750 mL
Chopped fresh dill (or 2 1/4 tsp., 11 mL, dried)	3 tbsp.	50 mL
Chopped cooked ham	3 cups	750 mL
Can of evaporated milk	6 oz.	170 mL
Chopped fresh dill (or 1 1/4 tsp., 6 mL, dried)	1 1/2 tbsp.	25 mL

Put zucchini and potato into 4 to 5 quart (4 to 5 L) slow cooker. Add flour. Toss gently until vegetables are coated.

Add next 3 ingredients. Stir. Cook, covered, on Low for 8 to 9 hours or on High for 4 to 4 1/2 hours. Cool slightly. Transfer about 3 cups (750 mL) vegetable mixture to blender or food processor using slotted spoon. Process until smooth (see Safety Tip). Return to slow cooker.

Add remaining 3 ingredients. Stir. Cook, covered, on High for about 15 minutes until heated through. Makes about 12 cups (3 L).

1 cup (250 mL): 181 Calories; 7.0 g Total Fat (2.9 g Mono, 0.9 g Poly, 2.5 g Sat); 33 mg Cholesterol; 17 g Carbohydrate; 2 g Fibre; 13 g Protein; 789 mg Sodium

Pictured on page 19.

Safety Tip: Follow manufacturer's instructions for processing hot liquids.

Curried Cauliflower Soup

Cooking oil	1 tbsp.	15 mL
Chopped onion	1 1/2 cups	375 mL
Chopped carrot	1 cup	250 mL
Chopped celery	1 cup	250 mL
Curry paste (or 1 tbsp., 15 mL, powder)	2 tbsp.	30 mL
Garlic cloves, minced (or 1/2 tsp., 2 mL, powder)	2	2
Prepared vegetable broth	5 cups	1.25 L
Medium peeled potatoes, cubed	2	2
Salt	1/4 tsp.	1 mL
Chopped cauliflower	2 1/2 cups	625 mL
Plain yogurt	1/2 cup	125 mL
Chopped fresh cilantro or parsley	2 tbsp.	30 mL

Heat cooking oil in large frying pan on medium. Add next 3 ingredients. Cook for 5 to 10 minutes, stirring often, until onion is softened.

Add curry paste and garlic. Heat and stir for about 1 minute until fragrant. Transfer to 3 1/2 to 4 quart (3.5 to 4 L) slow cooker.

Add next 3 ingredients. Stir. Cook, covered, on Low for 8 to 10 hours or on High for 4 to 5 hours. Carefully process with hand blender or in blender until smooth (see Safety Tip).

Add cauliflower and yogurt. Stir. Cook, covered, on High for about 45 minutes until cauliflower is tender-crisp.

Add cilantro. Stir. Makes about 8 cups (2 L).

1 cup (250 mL): 126 Calories; 3.8 g Total Fat (1.3 g Mono, 0.6 g Poly, 1.0 g Sat); 3 mg Cholesterol; 20 g Carbohydrate; 3 g Fibre; 3 g Protein; 537 mg Sodium

Pictured on page 17.

Safety Tip: Follow manufacturer's instructions for processing hot liquids.

Dare to make something deliciously different for dinner! The quaint combination of cauliflower and curry makes for a colourful and spicy soup.

about overcooking

Just because food can cook safely for hours in a slow cooker doesn't mean you can leave your recipe cooking for a couple extra hours with no dire effects. If you're cooking on the low setting, you can usually get away with an extra hour or possibly two—maximum! But going over the allotted time when cooking on the high setting will definitely overcook and possibly dry out your food. Most of our recipes have both a low and high-temperature cooking option, so if you think you're going to be running late, opt for the low setting.

You'll have more time to dance around the sombrero while this little fiesta of flavour is heating things up in your slow cooker. Serve with nacho chips.

Tex-Mex Taco Soup

Cooking oil	2 tsp.	10 mL
Lean ground beef	1 lb.	454 g
Prepared beef broth	6 cups	1.5 L
Can of kidney beans, rinsed and drained	19 oz.	540 mL
Chopped red onion	2 cups	500 mL
Can of diced tomatoes (with juice)	14 oz.	398 mL
Chopped celery	1 1/2 cups	375 mL
Grated carrot	1 1/2 cups	375 mL
Chopped green pepper	1 cup	250 mL
Chunky salsa	1 cup	250 mL
Brown sugar, packed	1 tsp.	5 mL
Dried basil	1 tsp.	5 mL
Chopped fresh parsley (or 3/4 tsp., 4 mL, flakes)	1 tbsp.	15 mL
Sour cream	1/2 cup	125 mL
Grated Monterey Jack cheese	1/2 cup	125 mL

Heat cooking oil in large frying pan on medium. Add beef. Scramble-fry for about 10 minutes until no longer pink. Drain. Transfer to 5 to 7 quart (5 to 7 L) slow cooker.

Add next 10 ingredients. Stir. Cook, covered, on Low for 8 to 10 hours or on High for 4 to 5 hours.

Add parsley. Stir.

Spoon sour cream and sprinkle cheese on individual servings. Makes about 14 cups (3.5 L).

1 cup (250 mL): 281 Calories; 7.1 g Total Fat (2.2 g Mono, 1.0 g Poly, 3.0 g Sat); 26 mg Cholesterol; 37 g Carbohydrate; 7 g Fibre; 19 g Protein; 581 mg Sodium

Pictured at right.

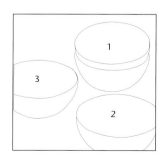

1. Pasta e Fagioli, page 24
2. Tex-Mex Taco Soup, above
3. Squash And Lentil Soup, page 25

Pasta e Fagioli

Bacon slices, diced	6	6
Chopped onion	1 cup	250 mL
Sliced carrot	1 cup	250 mL
Sliced celery	1 cup	250 mL
Garlic cloves, minced (or 1/2 tsp., 2 mL, powder)	2	2
Dried basil	1 tsp.	5 mL
Dried oregano	1 tsp.	5 mL
Pepper	1/2 tsp.	2 mL
Can of white kidney beans, rinsed and drained	19 oz.	540 mL
Can of diced tomatoes (with juice)	28 oz.	796 mL
Prepared chicken broth	3 cups	750 mL
Water	1 cup	250 mL
Tomato paste (see Tip)	1/4 cup	60 mL
Bay leaves	2	2
Water	5 cups	1.25 L
Salt	1/2 tsp.	2 mL
Tubetti	1 cup	250 mL
Chopped fresh parsley	2 tbsp.	30 mL
Grated Parmesan cheese	1/4 cup	60 mL

Cook bacon in medium frying pan on medium until crisp. Transfer to 4 to 5 quart (4 to 5 L) slow cooker using slotted spoon.

Heat 2 tsp. (10 mL) drippings in same frying pan on medium. Add next 7 ingredients. Cook for 5 to 10 minutes, stirring often, until onion is softened. Add to slow cooker.

Measure 1 cup (250 mL) beans onto plate. Mash with fork. Add to slow cooker. Add next 5 ingredients and remaining beans. Stir. Cook, covered, on Low for 7 to 8 hours or on High for 3 1/2 to 4 hours. Discard bay leaves.

Combine water and salt in large saucepan. Bring to a boil. Add tubetti. Boil, uncovered, for 10 to 12 minutes, stirring occasionally, until tender but firm. Drain. Add to slow cooker.

Add parsley. Stir.

(continued on next page)

Sprinkle cheese on individual servings. Makes about 12 cups (3 L).

1 cup (250 mL): 208 Calories; 5.9 g Total Fat (1.9 g Mono, 0.4 g Poly, 2.7 g Sat); 12 mg Cholesterol; 28 g Carbohydrate; 3 g Fibre; 12 g Protein; 854 mg Sodium

Pictured on page 23.

Squash And Lentil Soup

This velvety soup is a smooth operator with the mild sweetness of squash, the spiciness of ginger and curry, and the tang of yogurt.

Cooking oil	2 tsp.	10 mL
Chopped onion	2 cups	500 mL
Garlic cloves, minced	2	2
(or 1/2 tsp., 2 mL, powder)		
Finely grated gingerroot	1 tsp.	5 mL
(or 1/4 tsp., 1 mL, ground ginger)		
Curry powder	1 tbsp.	15 mL
Prepared chicken broth	6 cups	1.5 L
Chopped butternut squash	5 cups	1.25 L
(about 1/2 lbs., 680 g)		
Dried red split lentils	1 1/2 cups	375 mL
Plain yogurt	1/3 cup	75 mL

Heat cooking oil in large frying pan on medium. Add next 3 ingredients. Cook for 5 to 10 minutes, stirring often, until onion is softened.

Add curry powder. Heat and stir for 1 to 2 minutes until fragrant. Transfer to 4 to 5 quart (4 to 5 L) slow cooker.

Add next 3 ingredients. Stir. Cook, covered, on Low for 6 to 8 hours or on High for 3 to 4 hours until lentils and squash are tender. Carefully process with hand blender or in blender until smooth (see Safety Tip).

Add yogurt. Stir. Cook, covered, on High for about 15 minutes until heated through. Makes about 9 1/2 cups (2.4 L).

1 cup (250 mL): 213 Calories; 3.0 g Total Fat (1.0 g Mono, 0.6 g Poly, 0.6 g Sat); 2 mg Cholesterol; 38 g Carbohydrate; 8 g Fibre; 11 g Protein; 951 mg Sodium

Pictured on page 23.

Safety Tip: Follow manufacturer's instructions for processing hot liquids.

Tender pork and diced vegetables add a great deal of substance to this spicy soup. Although it takes a little time to prepare, the results are worth it! Serve with ciabatta bread or hot cornbread.

food fun

It's not called "jerk" because an unlikeable guy invented it. Jerk-style cooking actually comes from Jamaica. There are usually two components to jerk cooking—the spices and the cooking method. The spices are generally used as a meat rub, and combine to form a spicy, yet sweet flavour. The cooking style is usually slow barbecuing over an open fire—as evidenced by the outdoor jerk stands that are found scattered throughout busy Jamaican streets.

Jazzy Jerk Soup

Cooking oil	2 tbsp.	30 mL
Boneless pork loin chops, cut into 1/2 inch (12 mm) thick slices	1 lb.	454 g
Finely grated gingerroot (or 3/4 tsp., 4 mL, ground ginger)	1 tbsp.	15 mL
Paprika	2 tsp.	10 mL
Salt	1 1/2 tsp.	7 mL
Dried crushed chilies	3/4 tsp.	4 mL
Dried thyme	1/2 tsp.	2 mL
Ground cinnamon	1/4 tsp.	1 mL
Ground allspice	1/8 tsp.	0.5 mL
Coarsely ground pepper, sprinkle		
Ground cloves, sprinkle		
Chopped onion	1 cup	250 mL
Garlic clove, minced (or 1/4 tsp., 1 mL, powder)	1	1
Prepared chicken broth	1 cup	250 mL
Prepared chicken broth	3 cups	750 mL
Diced peeled potato	2 cups	500 mL
Diced peeled sweet potato	2 cups	500 mL
Diced yellow turnip	2 cups	500 mL
Can of cream-style corn	14 oz.	398 mL
Can of stewed tomatoes (with juice), coarsely chopped (see Note)	14 oz.	398 mL
Sliced carrot	1 cup	250 mL
Coarsely shredded fresh spinach leaves, lightly packed	2 cups	500 mL

Heat cooking oil in large frying pan on medium-high. Add next 10 ingredients. Cook for about 10 minutes, stirring occasionally, until pork is browned.

Add onion and garlic. Cook for 2 minutes, stirring occasionally. Stir in first amount of broth, scraping any brown bits from bottom of pan. Transfer to 4 to 5 quart (4 to 5 L) slow cooker.

Add next 7 ingredients. Stir. Cook, covered, on Low for 7 to 8 hours or on High for 3 1/2 to 4 hours.

(continued on next page)

Add spinach. Stir. Cook, covered, on High for about 5 minutes until spinach is wilted. Makes about 12 cups (3 L).

1 cup (250 mL): 178 Calories; 4.6 g Total Fat (2.3 g Mono, 1.2 g Poly, 0.9 g Sat); 24 mg Cholesterol; 25 g Carbohydrate; 3 g Fibre; 11 g Protein; 1014 mg Sodium

Pictured below.

Note: Cut tomatoes with a paring knife or kitchen shears while still in the can.

Left: Cock-A-Leekie, page 28
Right: Jazzy Jerk Soup, page 26

You needn't search the Scottish moors for a taste of traditional fare. Sound the bagpipes—this soup comes straight from the Highlands to your slow cooker. And although the name seems a bit nonsensical, it's actually derived from its traditional ingredients: rooster and leeks.

Cock-A-Leekie

Bacon slices, diced	4	4
Sliced leek (white part only)	4 cups	1 L
Pearl barley	1/2 cup	125 mL
Chopped carrot	1 cup	250 mL
Chopped celery	1/2 cup	125 mL
Bone-in chicken parts, skin removed (see Note)	3 1/2 lbs.	1.6 kg
Prepared chicken broth	7 cups	1.75 L
PEPPER BOUQUET GARNI		
Whole black peppercorns	8	8
Sprigs of fresh parsley	4	4
Sprig of fresh thyme	1	1
Bay leaf	1	1
Can of evaporated milk	3 3/4 oz.	110 mL
All-purpose flour	1 tbsp.	15 mL

Cook bacon in large frying pan on medium for about 5 minutes until almost crisp.

Add leek. Cook for about 5 minutes, stirring occasionally, until leek starts to soften. Transfer to 5 to 7 quart (5 to 7 L) slow cooker.

Layer next 4 ingredients, in order given, over leek mixture. Pour broth over chicken.

Pepper Bouquet Garni: Place first 4 ingredients on 10 inch (25 cm) square piece of cheesecloth. Draw up corners and tie with string. Submerge in liquid in slow cooker. Cook, covered, on Low for 8 to 10 hours or on High for 4 to 5 hours. Remove and discard bouquet garni. Transfer chicken to cutting board using slotted spoon. Remove chicken from bones. Discard bones. Cut chicken into bite-sized pieces. Return to slow cooker.

Whisk evaporated milk into flour in small bowl until smooth. Add to soup. Stir well. Cook, covered, on High for about 5 minutes until boiling and slightly thickened. Makes about 12 cups (3 L).

1 cup (250 mL): 270 Calories; 8.5 g Total Fat (3.9 g Mono, 2.0 g Poly, 3.3 g Sat); 98 mg Cholesterol; 15 g Carbohydrate; 2 g Fibre; 32 g Protein; 1043 mg Sodium

Pictured on page 27.

Note: Use whichever cuts of chicken you prefer as long as the weight used is equal to that listed.

Split Pea Soup

Water	5 cups	1.25 L
Green split peas, rinsed and drained	2 cups	500 mL
Finely chopped onion	1 cup	250 mL
Can of flaked ham (with liquid), broken up (or 1 cup, 250 mL, diced cooked ham)	6.5 oz.	184 g
Diced celery	1/2 cup	125 mL
Medium carrot, thinly sliced	1	1
Chicken bouillon powder	1 tbsp.	15 mL
Parsley flakes	1 tsp.	5 mL
Ground thyme	1/4 tsp.	1 mL
Salt	1/2 tsp.	2 mL
Pepper	1/4 tsp.	1 mL

Combine all 11 ingredients in 3 1/2 to 4 quart (3.5 to 4 L) slow cooker. Cook, covered, on Low for 8 to 10 hours or on High for 4 to 5 hours. Makes about 8 cups (2 L).

1 cup (250 mL): 207 Calories; 2.9 g Total Fat (0.9 g Mono, 0.2 g Poly, 0.6 g Sat); 11 mg Cholesterol; 28 g Carbohydrate; 5 g Fibre; 16 g Protein; 816 mg Sodium

The trick to a good split pea soup is giving it time to properly simmer and blend its flavours—and there's no better way to do that than in a slow cooker.

Without our slow cookers we'd certainly swoon! This traditional Southern fave, in soup form, will leave all the beaus and belles feeling satisfied.

Chicken And Dumpling Soup

Chopped onion	1/2 cup	125 mL
Chopped peeled potato	1 cup	250 mL
Chopped carrot	1 cup	250 mL
Shredded green cabbage, lightly packed	1 cup	250 mL
Small fresh whole white mushrooms, halved	1 cup	250 mL
Boneless, skinless chicken thighs, cut into 1 inch (2.5 cm) pieces	1 lb.	454 g
Prepared chicken broth	2 cups	500 mL
Can of condensed cream of mushroom soup	10 oz.	284 mL
Dried rosemary, crushed	1/4 tsp.	1 mL
Dried thyme	1/4 tsp.	1 mL
Paprika	1/4 tsp.	1 mL
Pepper	1/4 tsp.	1 mL
Bay leaf	1	1
ROSEMARY DUMPLINGS		
All-purpose flour	1 cup	250 mL
Grated Parmesan cheese	2 tbsp.	30 mL
Baking powder	1 tsp.	5 mL
Dried rosemary, crushed	1/8 tsp.	0.5 mL
Large egg, fork-beaten	1	1
Buttermilk (or soured milk, see Tip)	3 tbsp.	50 mL
Cooking oil	2 tbsp.	30 mL

Layer first 6 ingredients, in order given, in 3 1/2 to 4 quart (3.5 to 4 L) slow cooker.

Combine next 6 ingredients in small bowl. Pour over chicken. Add bay leaf. Cook, covered, on Low for 6 hours or on High for 3 hours. Discard bay leaf. Stir. Bring to a boil on High. Makes about 6 cups (1.5 L).

Rosemary Dumplings: Measure first 4 ingredients into medium bowl. Stir. Make a well in centre.

(continued on next page)

Combine remaining 3 ingredients in small bowl. Add to well. Stir until just moistened. Spoon mounds of batter, using 1 tbsp. (15 mL) for each, in single layer over soup. Cook, covered, on High for about 30 minutes until wooden pick inserted in centre of dumpling comes out clean. Serves 6.

1 serving: 368 Calories; 17.4 g Total Fat (6.3 g Mono, 3.0 g Poly, 4.8 g Sat); 91 mg Cholesterol; 30 g Carbohydrate; 2 g Fibre; 23 g Protein; 1147 mg Sodium

Pictured below.

This richly flavoured side has all the delicious essence and creamy texture of a traditional rice risotto—but it's made with barley.

Herbed Barley Risotto

Cooking oil	1 tbsp.	15 mL
Finely chopped onion	1 cup	250 mL
Sliced fresh white mushrooms	2 cups	500 mL
Garlic cloves, minced (or 1 tsp., 5 mL, powder)	4	4
Prepared vegetable broth	2 2/3 cups	650 mL
Medium tomatoes, peeled (see Tip), quartered, seeds removed	3	3
Pearl barley	1 cup	250 mL
Dry (or alcohol-free) white wine	1/2 cup	125 mL
Dried oregano	1/2 tsp.	2 mL
Dried rosemary, crushed	1/2 tsp.	2 mL
Salt	1/4 tsp.	1 mL
Pepper	1/4 tsp.	1 mL
Grated Parmesan cheese	1/3 cup	75 mL
Chopped fresh parsley	2 tbsp.	30 mL

Heat cooking oil in medium frying pan on medium. Add onion. Cook for 5 to 10 minutes, stirring often, until softened.

Add mushrooms and garlic. Cook for 3 to 5 minutes, stirring occasionally, until mushrooms are softened. Transfer to 3 1/2 to 4 quart (3.5 to 4 L) slow cooker.

Add next 8 ingredients. Stir. Cook, covered, on Low for 8 to 9 hours or on High for 4 to 4 1/2 hours.

Add cheese and parsley. Stir. Makes about 4 cups (1 L).

1 cup (250 mL): 343 Calories; 7.5 g Total Fat (2.1 g Mono, 1.3 g Poly, 1.7 g Sat); 7 mg Cholesterol; 54 g Carbohydrate; 6 g Fibre; 12 g Protein; 634 mg Sodium

Pictured at right.

Left: Slow Cooker Dolmades, page 34
Top Right: Herbed Barley Risotto, above

Dolmades
P 34

Dolmades (pronounced dohl-MAH-dehs) are the Greek equivalent of the cabbage roll. Grape leaves, available in the import section of your grocery store, are rolled around a flavourful filling of rice, lamb, mint and raisins. Garnish with lemon wedges or a curl of lemon zest and serve with tzatziki or plain yogurt.

food fun

Did you know that purple, brown and yellow raisins all come from the same grape? The way a raisin is dried will determine its colour. In North America, most raisins are made from Thompson Seedless grapes. Dark purple/black raisins are sun-dried, light/medium brown raisins have been mechanically dehydrated, and gold/yellow raisins have been mechanically dehydrated and treated with sulphur dioxide. Sulphur dioxide is used on many dried fruits and prevents light-coloured fruits from darkening.

Slow Cooker Dolmades

Ingredient	Imperial	Metric
Water	2 1/2 cups	625 mL
Salt	1 tsp.	5 mL
Basmati (or long grain) white rice	1 3/4 cups	425 mL
Olive (or cooking) oil	1 tbsp.	15 mL
Diced onion	1 1/2 cups	375 mL
Lean ground lamb	1 lb.	454 g
Garlic cloves, minced	3	3
(or 3/4 tsp., 4 mL, powder)		
Dried mint leaves	1 tsp.	5 mL
Dried oregano	1 tsp.	5 mL
Parsley flakes	1 tsp.	5 mL
Salt	1 tsp.	5 mL
Pepper	1/4 tsp.	1 mL
Raisins, chopped (optional)	1/2 cup	125 mL
Jars of grape leaves (17 oz., 473 mL, each), rinsed and drained, tough stems removed (see Note)	2	2
Boiling water	4 1/3 cups	1.1 L
Lemon juice	1/2 cup	125 mL
Olive (or cooking) oil	3 tbsp.	50 mL
Garlic cloves, halved	4	4
(or 1/4 tsp., 1 mL, powder)		
Granulated sugar	1/2 tsp.	2 mL

Combine water and salt in medium saucepan. Bring to a boil. Add rice. Stir. Reduce heat to medium-low. Simmer, covered, for about 12 minutes until liquid is absorbed and rice is almost tender. Cool. Fluff with fork.

Heat first amount of olive oil in large frying pan. Add onion. Cook for 5 to 10 minutes, stirring often, until softened.

Add lamb and first amount of garlic. Scramble-fry for about 5 minutes until lamb is no longer pink. Drain. Transfer to large bowl.

Add next 6 ingredients and rice. Stir well.

(continued on next page)

Place grape leaves on work surface, vein-side up, stem-side (bottom of leaf) closest to you. Line bottom of 5 quart (5 L) slow cooker with a few small or torn leaves. Place 1 to 2 tbsp. (15 to 30 mL) lamb mixture about 1/2 inch (12 mm) from bottom of leaf. Fold bottom of leaf over lamb mixture. Fold in sides. Roll up from bottom to enclose filling. Do not roll too tightly as rice will expand. Repeat with remaining leaves and lamb mixture. Arrange rolls, seam-side down, close together in layers over leaves in slow cooker. Separate layers with small or torn leaves. Place any remaining leaves over top.

Combine remaining 5 ingredients in medium bowl. Slowly pour over dolmades, allowing all air spaces to fill, until water mixture is just visible on sides. Set aside any remaining water mixture. Cook, covered, on Low for 3 1/2 to 4 hours, checking after 2 1/2 hours and adding more water mixture if necessary. Turn off slow cooker. Let stand, covered, for at least 30 minutes to allow rolls to set. Drain and discard any remaining liquid. Carefully transfer dolmades to large serving platter. Cool. Serve at room temperature. Store any remaining rolls in airtight containers in freezer for up to 1 month. Makes about 75 dolmades.

1 dolmade: 49 Calories; 2.4 g Total Fat (1.1 g Mono, 0.3 g Poly, 0.8 g Sat); 4 mg Cholesterol; 5 g Carbohydrate; trace Fibre; 2 g Protein; 433 mg Sodium

Pictured on page 33.

Note: Choose the best grape leaves for rolling and save the smaller or torn leaves for separating layers and lining the bottom of the slow cooker.

Got a big batch of people coming for dinner? Well, this big batch of creamy, tangy potatoes will satisfy everyone's starch cravings—not to mention free up the oven for your entree.

Make-Ahead Potatoes

Medium peeled potatoes, quartered	9	9
Block of light cream cheese, softened and cut up	8 oz.	250 g
Light sour cream	1 cup	250 mL
Dried chives	1 tbsp.	15 mL
Parsley flakes	1 tsp.	5 mL
Onion powder	1/2 tsp.	2 mL
Garlic powder	1/4 tsp.	1 mL
Salt	1 tsp.	5 mL
Pepper	1/4 tsp.	1 mL

Pour water into large saucepan or Dutch oven until about 1 inch (2.5 cm) deep. Add potato. Cover. Bring to a boil. Reduce heat to medium. Boil gently for 12 to 15 minutes until tender. Drain. Mash.

Beat remaining 8 ingredients in medium bowl until combined. Add to potato. Mix well. Transfer to greased 3 1/2 to 4 quart (3.5 to 4 L) slow cooker. Cook, covered, on Low for 6 to 8 hours or on High for 3 to 4 hours, stirring occasionally. Makes about 8 cups (2 L).

1 cup (250 mL): 264 Calories; 7.1 g Total Fat (0 g Mono, 0.1 g Poly, 4.7 g Sat); 23 mg Cholesterol; 42 g Carbohydrate; 3 g Fibre; 8 g Protein; 455 mg Sodium

All dressed up and no place to go? Never! These baby red potatoes, adorned with an irresistibly creamy dressing, are heading straight to your dinner plate.

variation

If you want to up the flavour factor of Dressed Red Potatoes, use half an envelope of ranch dressing mix and half an envelope of dill dressing mix instead of just one or the other.

Dressed Red Potatoes

Red baby potatoes, cut in half	2 1/2 lbs.	1.1 kg
Can of condensed cream of potato soup	10 oz.	284 mL
Block of light cream cheese, softened and cut up	8 oz.	250 g
Envelope of buttermilk dill (or ranch) dressing mix	1 oz.	28 g
Parsley flakes	1 tsp.	5 mL

Put potato into 3 1/2 to 4 quart (3.5 to 4 L) slow cooker.

Beat remaining 4 ingredients in medium bowl until combined. Spoon over potato. Cook, covered, on Low for 6 to 7 hours or on High for 3 to 3 1/2 hours. Makes about 9 1/2 cups (2.4 L).

1 cup (250 mL): 223 Calories; 4.5 g Total Fat (0.1 g Mono, 0.2 g Poly, 2.9 g Sat); 13 mg Cholesterol; 25 g Carbohydrate; 2 g Fibre; 5 g Protein; 685 mg Sodium

Lentil Potato Mash

Red baby potatoes, larger ones cut in half	1 lb.	454 g
Prepared vegetable broth	1 3/4 cups	425 mL
Can of light coconut milk	14 oz.	398 mL
Chopped onion	1 cup	250 mL
Chopped peeled sweet potato	1 cup	250 mL
Dried red split lentils	1 cup	250 mL
Smooth peanut butter	1/4 cup	60 mL
Curry powder	2 tsp.	10 mL
Soy sauce	2 tsp.	10 mL
Finely grated gingerroot	1 tsp.	5 mL
(or 1/4 tsp., 1 mL, ground ginger)		
Garlic clove, minced	1	1
(or 1/4 tsp., 1 mL, powder)		
Chili paste (sambal oelek)	1/2 tsp.	2 mL
Granulated sugar	1/2 tsp.	2 mL
Salt	1/2 tsp.	2 mL
Chopped fresh parsley	1 tbsp.	15 mL

Combine first 14 ingredients in 3 1/2 quart (3.5 L) slow cooker. Cook, covered, on Low for 7 to 8 hours or on High for 3 1/2 to 4 hours. Mash. Transfer to serving bowl.

Sprinkle with parsley. Makes about 5 1/2 cups (1.4 L).

1 cup (250 mL): 351 Calories; 11.9 g Total Fat (2.9 g Mono, 1.7 g Poly, 4.8 g Sat); 0 mg Cholesterol; 47 g Carbohydrate; 9 g Fibre; 15 g Protein; 498 mg Sodium

This delightful curried mash of lentils, potatoes and sweet potatoes is a sure winner. If you don't like potato skins in your mash, make sure to peel the baby potatoes.

about coconut milk

Contrary to what one would expect, coconut milk is not the liquid found inside a coconut. The juice inside the coconut is quite watery and wouldn't lend the same rich, creamy texture to Asian, African and Polynesian dishes that coconut milk does. The canned coconut milk you buy at the store comes from squeezing juice out of the actual meat of the coconut.

There will be no suffering involved when you tuck into this creamy southern staple.

Sufferin' Succotash

Frozen kernel corn	2 cups	500 mL
Frozen lima beans	2 cups	500 mL
Chopped onion	1 1/2 cups	375 mL
Can of condensed cream of mushroom soup	10 oz.	284 mL
Sliced celery	1/2 cup	125 mL
Jar of sliced pimiento, chopped	2 oz.	57 mL
Dried basil	1/4 tsp.	1 mL
Garlic powder	1/4 tsp.	1 mL
Salt	1/2 tsp.	2 mL
Pepper	1/8 tsp.	0.5 mL
Grated medium Cheddar cheese	1/3 cup	75 mL

Combine first 10 ingredients in 3 1/2 quart (3.5 L) slow cooker. Cook, covered, on Low for 8 to 10 hours or on High for 4 to 5 hours. Stir. Transfer to serving bowl.

Sprinkle with cheese. Makes about 4 cups (1 L).

1 cup (250 mL): 296 Calories; 8.0 g Total Fat (0.9 g Mono, 0.3 g Poly, 3.0 g Sat); 13 mg Cholesterol; 46 g Carbohydrate; 7 g Fibre; 12 g Protein; 918 mg Sodium

Pictured at right.

A perfect side is as easy as a medley of carrots and onions. The slow cooking allows the natural flavours to really come through. Use a crinkle cutter on the carrots for a showier presentation.

Carrot Onion Bake

Diagonally sliced carrot	6 cups	1.5 L
Sliced onion	1 1/2 cups	375 mL
Water	1/2 cup	125 mL
Salt	1/2 tsp.	2 mL
SAUCE		
All-purpose flour	1 tbsp.	15 mL
Salt, sprinkle		
Pepper, sprinkle		
Milk	1/2 cup	125 mL
Grated medium (or sharp) Cheddar cheese	1/2 cup	125 mL
TOPPING		
Butter (or hard margarine)	1 tbsp.	15 mL
Fine dry bread crumbs	1/4 cup	60 mL

(continued on next page)

Combine first 4 ingredients in 3 1/2 to 4 quart (3.5 to 4 L) slow cooker. Cook, covered, on High for 4 to 5 hours. Drain. Transfer to serving bowl. Cover to keep warm.

Sauce: Combine first 3 ingredients in small saucepan. Slowly add milk, stirring constantly with whisk, until smooth. Heat and stir on medium until boiling and thickened.

Add cheese. Heat and stir until cheese is melted. Add to vegetable mixture. Stir.

Topping: Melt butter in separate small saucepan on medium. Add bread crumbs. Heat and stir until crumbs are browned. Sprinkle over vegetable mixture. Makes about 6 cups (1.5 L).

1 cup (250 mL): 155 Calories; 5.8 g Total Fat (1.6 g Mono, 0.4 g Poly, 3.4 g Sat); 16 mg Cholesterol; 22 g Carbohydrate; 4 g Fibre; 5 g Protein; 211 mg Sodium

Pictured below.

Left: Carrot Onion Bake, page 38
Right: Sufferin' Succotash, page 38

Fruity Beans And Sausage

The smoky flavour of the sausage in this dish is contrasted by the unexpected sweet and fruity aftertaste. Serve over couscous for a pretty presentation.

Can of chickpeas (garbanzo beans), rinsed and drained	19 oz.	540 mL
Can of baked beans in molasses	14 oz.	398 mL
Can of pineapple tidbits, drained and juice reserved	14 oz.	398 mL
Can of red kidney beans, rinsed and drained	14 oz.	398 mL
Smoked ham sausage, cut into 1/4 inch (6 mm) slices	1/2 lb.	225 g
Medium unpeeled cooking apple (such as McIntosh), diced	1	1
Chopped onion	1/2 cup	125 mL
Apple cider vinegar	2 tbsp.	30 mL
Fancy (mild) molasses	2 tbsp.	30 mL
Dry mustard	1 tsp.	5 mL
Reserved pineapple juice (optional)	2 tbsp.	30 mL
Cornstarch (optional)	1 tbsp.	15 mL

Combine first 10 ingredients in 3 1/2 to 4 quart (3.5 to 4 L) slow cooker. Cook, covered, on Low for 6 to 7 hours or on High for 3 to 3 1/2 hours.

Stir pineapple juice into cornstarch in small cup. Add to slow cooker. Stir. Cook, covered, on High for about 5 minutes until boiling and slightly thickened. Makes about 7 cups (1.75 L).

1 cup (250 mL): 317 Calories; 6.1 g Total Fat (0.4 g Mono, 0.6 g Poly, 0.2 g Sat); 2 mg Cholesterol; 50 g Carbohydrate; 11 g Fibre; 16 g Protein; 726 mg Sodium

Pictured at right.

Sweet Bean Pot

This medley of beans gets its uniquely sweet and tangy taste from sweet Spanish onions, brown sugar and cider vinegar. A bean lover's delight!

Bacon slices, diced	8	8
Thinly sliced Spanish onion	1 1/2 cups	375 mL
Garlic cloves, minced (or 1/2 tsp., 2 mL, powder)	2	2
Brown sugar, packed	1 cup	250 mL
Apple cider vinegar	1/2 cup	125 mL
Dry mustard	1 tsp.	5 mL
Salt	1/2 tsp.	2 mL

(continued on next page)

Cans of baked beans in tomato sauce (14 oz., 398 mL, each)	2	2
Can of lima beans, rinsed and drained	19 oz.	540 mL
Can of pinto beans, rinsed and drained	19 oz.	540 mL
Can of red kidney beans, rinsed and drained	19 oz.	540 mL
Can of white kidney beans, rinsed and drained	19 oz.	540 mL

Cook bacon in medium frying pan on medium until almost crisp. Drain all but 2 tbsp. (30 mL) drippings.

Add onion. Cook for 5 to 10 minutes, stirring often, until onion is softened and bacon is crisp.

Add garlic. Heat and stir for 1 to 2 minutes until fragrant.

Add next 4 ingredients. Stir. Bring to a boil.

Put remaining 5 ingredients into 4 to 5 quart (4 to 5 L) slow cooker. Add bacon mixture. Stir. Cook, covered, on Low for 6 hours or on High for 3 hours. Makes about 10 cups (2.5 L).

1 cup (250 mL): 390 Calories; 5.9 g Total Fat (2.2 g Mono, 1.0 g Poly, 1.7 g Sat); 12 mg Cholesterol; 70 g Carbohydrate; 14 g Fibre; 16 g Protein; 1001 mg Sodium

about brown sugar

So what's the difference between brown sugar and white sugar? Brown sugar is actually white sugar that has had molasses added to it. The molasses gives it its soft texture, rich colour and characteristic taste. Brown sugar will get hard if it loses its moisture, so to rehydrate, place a small amount in a microwave-safe bowl and set side by side with a bowl of water in the microwave. Microwave on high for approximately one minute until soft.

Fruity Beans And Sausage, page 40

Applesauce

Medium cooking apples (such as McIntosh), peeled and sliced	8	8
Water	1/2 cup	125 mL
Granulated sugar	1/2 cup	125 mL

Combine apple and water in 3 1/2 quart (3.5 L) slow cooker. Cook, covered, on Low for 4 to 5 hours or on High for 2 to 2 1/2 hours.

Sprinkle sugar over top. Stir. Makes about 4 cups (1 L).

1/2 cup (125 mL): 108 Calories; 0.2 g Total Fat (trace Mono, 0.1 g Poly, trace Sat); 0 mg Cholesterol; 28 g Carbohydrate; 2 g Fibre; trace Protein; trace Sodium

Pictured on page 45.

Cranberry Sauce

Granulated sugar	2 cups	500 mL
Boiling water	1 cup	250 mL
Fresh (or frozen) cranberries	4 cups	1 L

Combine sugar and water in 3 1/2 quart (3.5 L) slow cooker.

Add cranberries. Stir. Cook, covered, on High for about 1 1/2 hours until cranberries are split. Sauce will thicken as it cools. Makes about 3 1/2 cups (875 mL).

2 tbsp. (30 mL): 60 Calories; 0 g Total Fat (0 g Mono, 0 g Poly, 0 g Sat); 0 mg Cholesterol; 15 g Carbohydrate; 1 g Fibre; 0 g Protein; trace Sodium

Pictured on page 45.

Stuffing

Hot water	1 1/2 cups	375 mL
Butter (or hard margarine)	1/4 cup	60 mL
Chicken bouillon powder	1 tbsp.	15 mL
Parsley flakes	1 tbsp.	15 mL
Poultry seasoning	2 tsp.	10 mL
Salt	1 tsp.	5 mL
Pepper	1/4 tsp.	1 mL
Dry white bread cubes	10 cups	2.5 L
Chopped celery	1 cup	250 mL
Chopped onion	1 cup	250 mL

If the oven's already stuffed with turkey, stuff this flavourful dressing into your slow cooker instead.

Measure first 7 ingredients into extra-large heatproof bowl. Stir until butter is melted.

Add remaining 3 ingredients. Toss until coated. Transfer to greased 3 1/2 to 4 quart (3.5 to 4 L) slow cooker. Cook, covered, on Low for 5 to 6 hours (see Note). Makes about 8 cups (2 L).

1/2 cup (125 mL): 91 Calories; 3.6 g Total Fat (0.9 g Mono, 0.4 g Poly, 2.0 g Sat); 8 mg Cholesterol; 13 g Carbohydrate; 1 g Fibre; 2 g Protein; 532 mg Sodium

Note: If you prefer a more moist stuffing, add a bit more hot water while cooking. Stir.

Jalapeño peppers add an unexpected kick to this scrumptious stuffing.

tip

Pickled jalapeño peppers are still hot peppers, so wear rubber gloves when handling and avoid touching your eyes—and always wash your hands well afterwards.

tip

Greasing your slow cooker with butter before adding your stuffing makes cleanup easier. It also gives your stuffing a nice flavour with crisp, browned edges.

Spicy Sausage And Bread Stuffing

Package of frozen sausage meat, thawed	13 oz.	375 g
Herb (or garlic) seasoned croutons	10 cups	2.5 L
Finely chopped sliced pickled jalapeño peppers (see Tip)	2 tbsp.	30 mL
Butter (or hard margarine)	1/2 cup	125 mL
Chopped celery (with leaves)	2 cups	500 mL
Chopped onion	2 cups	500 mL
Chopped fresh parsley (or 2 tbsp., 30 mL, flakes)	1/2 cup	125 mL
Dried sage	2 tsp.	10 mL
Dried oregano	1 tsp.	5 mL
Dried thyme	1 tsp.	5 mL
Pepper, sprinkle		
Can of condensed chicken broth	10 oz.	284 mL
Hot water, approximately	1/2 cup	125 mL
Butter (or hard margarine)	1 tbsp.	15 mL

Heat large frying pan on medium-high. Add sausage. Scramble-fry for about 10 minutes until browned. Drain. Transfer to extra-large bowl.

Add croutons and jalapeño pepper. Stir.

Melt first amount of butter in same frying pan on medium. Add celery and onion. Cook for about 10 minutes, stirring often, until softened.

Add next 5 ingredients. Stir. Add to sausage mixture. Stir.

Drizzle with broth and enough hot water until mixture holds together lightly.

Grease 3 1/2 to 4 quart (3.5 to 4 L) slow cooker with second amount of butter. Spoon stuffing into slow cooker. Pack down lightly. Cook, covered, on Low for about 2 hours until heated through. Makes about 8 cups (2 L).

1/2 cup (125 mL): 263 Calories; 17.9 g Total Fat (7.2 g Mono, 1.7 g Poly, 7.8 g Sat); 35 mg Cholesterol; 20 g Carbohydrate; 2 g Fibre; 6 g Protein; 659 mg Sodium

Pictured at right.

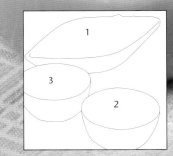

1. Spicy Sausage And Bread Stuffing, page 44
2. Cranberry Sauce, page 42
3. Applesauce, page 42

Imagine coming home to the inviting aroma of a hot pot roast dinner, complete with potatoes and vegetables. No scrambling or fuss to make dinner— simply pull out the plates.

pot roast gravy

To make a quick thick gravy for your Pot Roast, combine 2 tbsp. (30 mL) of flour, 1/4 tsp. (1 mL) of salt and a pinch of pepper in a small saucepan. On medium heat, slowly whisk in 1 cup (250 mL) of strained liquid from the Pot Roast. Keep stirring until the gravy is boiling and thickened. For a more flavourful gravy, you can add up to 1 tsp. (5 mL) of bouillon powder or a little more salt and pepper. Makes about 1 cup (250 mL).

Certainly not short on flavour, these short ribs are coated in a tangy barbecue sauce and are fall-off-the-bone tender.

Pot Roast

Medium peeled potatoes, quartered	4	4
Medium carrots, cut into 4 pieces each	4	4
Medium onions, cut into 8 wedges each	2	2
Boneless beef blade (or cross-rib) roast	3 lbs.	1.4 kg
Boiling water	1/2 cup	125 mL
Beef bouillon powder	1 tsp.	5 mL
Liquid gravy browner (optional)	1/2 tsp.	2 mL
Fresh (or frozen) whole green beans, halved	2 cups	500 mL

Layer first 3 ingredients, in order given, in 5 to 7 quart (5 to 7 L) slow cooker. Place roast over top.

Combine next 3 ingredients in small bowl. Pour over roast. Cook, covered, on Low for 10 to 12 hours or on High for 5 to 6 hours until roast is tender.

Add green beans. Cook, covered, on High for 15 to 20 minutes until tender-crisp. Transfer roast to cutting board. Cover with foil. Let stand for 10 minutes. Cut roast into thin slices. Transfer vegetables to serving bowl using slotted spoon. Serves 8.

1 serving: 468 Calories; 28.1 g Total Fat (12.0 g Mono, 1.1 g Poly, 11.1 g Sat); 115 mg Cholesterol; 22 g Carbohydrate; 4 g Fibre; 33 g Protein; 197 mg Sodium

Pictured on front cover and at right.

Barbecue Beef Ribs

Cooking oil	2 tbsp.	30 mL
Beef short ribs, bone-in, trimmed of fat	3 lbs.	1.4 kg
Barbecue sauce	1 cup	250 mL
Fancy (mild) molasses	2 tbsp.	30 mL
White vinegar	2 tbsp.	30 mL
Soy sauce	1 tbsp.	15 mL
Salt	1 1/2 tsp.	7 mL
Pepper	1/2 tsp.	2 mL
Chopped onion	1/2 cup	125 mL

(continued on next page)

Heat cooking oil in large frying pan on medium. Add ribs. Cook for about 5 minutes, turning occasionally, until browned on all sides. Transfer to 5 to 7 quart (5 to 7 L) slow cooker.

Combine next 6 ingredients in medium bowl.

Add onion. Stir. Pour over ribs. Cook, covered, on Low for 8 to 10 hours or on High for 4 to 5 hours. Serves 4.

1 serving: 748 Calories; 42.7 g Total Fat (19.4 g Mono, 3.8 g Poly, 15.4 g Sat); 163 mg Cholesterol; 18 g Carbohydrate; 4 g Fibre; 69 g Protein; 1847 mg Sodium

Pot Roast, page 46

Full of fresh herbs, this bean and beef stew has a hint of spring in it. Complete with fluffy, melt-in-your-mouth biscuits, this is wholesome cooking at its best.

tip

To make soured milk, measure 2 tsp. (10 mL) white vinegar or lemon juice into a 3/4 cup (175 mL) liquid measure, then add enough milk to make 3/4 cup (175 mL). Stir and let stand for 1 minute.

Beef And Biscuits

Stewing beef	2 lbs.	900 g
Can of diced tomatoes (with juice)	28 oz.	796 mL
Can of red kidney beans, rinsed and drained	19 oz.	540 mL
Chopped onion	1 cup	250 mL
Water	1/2 cup	125 mL
Chopped fresh oregano	2 tbsp.	30 mL
(or 1 1/2 tsp., 7 mL, dried)		
Beef bouillon powder	4 tsp.	20 mL
Chili powder	2 tsp.	10 mL
Granulated sugar	1 tsp.	5 mL
Ground coriander	3/4 tsp.	4 mL
Ground cumin	3/4 tsp.	4 mL
Salt	1/4 tsp.	1 mL

BISCUITS

All-purpose flour	1 1/2 cups	375 mL
Yellow cornmeal	1/2 cup	125 mL
Grated Parmesan cheese	1/3 cup	75 mL
Chopped fresh cilantro or parsley	2 tbsp.	30 mL
(or 1 1/2 tsp., 7 mL, dried)		
Baking powder	1 tbsp.	15 mL
Baking soda	1/2 tsp.	2 mL
Salt, just a pinch		
Pepper, just a pinch		
Cold butter (or hard margarine), cut up	3 tbsp.	50 mL
Buttermilk (or soured milk, see Tip), approximately	3/4 cup	175 mL

Combine first 12 ingredients in 4 to 5 quart (4 to 5 L) slow cooker. Cook, covered, on Low for 8 to 10 hours or on High for 4 to 5 hours. Bring to a boil on High. Makes about 6 1/2 cups (1.6 L).

Biscuits: Measure first 8 ingredients into large bowl. Stir. Cut in butter until mixture resembles coarse crumbs. Make a well in centre.

Add buttermilk to well. Stir until soft dough forms. Turn out onto lightly floured surface. Knead 8 times. Roll or pat out to 1/2 inch (12 mm) thickness. Cut out circles with lightly floured 2 inch (5 cm) biscuit cutter. Arrange biscuits, just touching, over beef mixture. Cook, covered, on High for about 30 minutes until wooden pick inserted in centre of biscuit comes out clean. Serves 8.

1 serving: 703 Calories; 21.5 g Total Fat (7.5 g Mono, 1.2 g Poly, 10.9 g Sat); 91 mg Cholesterol; 75 g Carbohydrate; 11 g Fibre; 53 g Protein; 1437 mg Sodium

Dijon Beef Stew

Baby carrots	1 lb.	454 g
Baby potatoes, larger ones cut in half	1 lb.	454 g
Chopped green pepper	1 1/4 cups	300 mL
Chopped onion	1 1/4 cups	300 mL
All-purpose flour	1/4 cup	60 mL
Paprika	1/4 tsp.	1 mL
Stewing beef	1 1/2 lbs.	680 g
Cooking oil	2 tsp.	10 mL
Prepared beef broth	1 1/2 cups	375 mL
Dijon mustard	1/3 cup	75 mL
Worcestershire sauce	2 tsp.	10 mL
Dried oregano	1/2 tsp.	2 mL
Chopped red pepper	3/4 cup	175 mL

Put first 4 ingredients into 4 to 5 quart (4 to 5 L) slow cooker.

Combine flour and paprika in large resealable freezer bag. Add beef. Seal bag. Toss until coated.

Heat cooking oil in large frying pan on medium. Add beef. Reserve remaining flour mixture. Cook for 5 to 10 minutes, stirring occasionally, until browned on all sides. Add to slow cooker.

Combine next 4 ingredients and remaining flour mixture in same frying pan. Heat and stir on medium until slightly thickened. Add to slow cooker. Stir. Cook, covered, on Low for 8 to 10 hours or on High for 4 to 5 hours.

Add red pepper. Stir. Cook, covered, on High for about 10 minutes until red pepper is tender-crisp. Makes about 8 cups (2 L).

1 cup (250 mL): 251 Calories; 8.9 g Total Fat (3.8 g Mono, 0.8 g Poly, 3.2 g Sat); 47 mg Cholesterol; 21 g Carbohydrate; 3 g Fibre; 21 g Protein; 405 mg Sodium

A healthy amount of Dijon gives this stew an interestingly piquant edge. Garnish with chopped fresh dill and serve with rolls or salad.

about dijon

Dijon mustard is aptly named after the city in France where it was invented. The original Dijon mustard was differentiated from other mustards because it used the juice from unripe grapes instead of the usual vinegar. This substitution resulted in a smoother, less-harsh mustard. Because Dijon has a smoother taste than prepared yellow mustard, it is inadvisable to substitute one for the other in recipes.

Perhaps one of our most often-requested slow cooker dishes, this beef delight gets rave reviews from people who have never liked corned beef before!

about corned beef

So what is corned beef anyway? It is simply beef that has been pickled in brine. The recipe for corned beef dates back many hundreds of years when people would brine their beef as a way of preserving it. The term "corned" actually relates to the coarse "corns" or grains of salt that were used in the brining process.

Corned Beef Dinner

Baby carrots	1 lb.	454 g
Red baby potatoes, larger ones cut in half	1 lb.	454 g
Medium yellow turnip, cut into 1 inch (2.5 cm) cubes	1	1
Chopped onion	2 cups	500 mL
Corned beef brisket	2 lbs.	900 g
Water	4 cups	1 L
Bay leaves	2	2
Whole black peppercorns	1 tbsp.	15 mL

Layer first 4 ingredients, in order given, in 5 to 7 quart (5 to 7 L) slow cooker. Place corned beef over onion, fat-side up.

Pour water over corned beef. Add bay leaves and peppercorns. Cook, covered, on Low for 8 to 10 hours or on High for 4 to 5 hours. Discard bay leaves. Transfer corned beef to large serving platter. Cut into thin slices. Transfer vegetables to serving bowl using slotted spoon. Serve with beef. Discard any remaining liquid in slow cooker. Serves 6.

1 serving: 310 Calories; 11.7 g Total Fat (5.5 g Mono, 0.6 g Poly, 3.8 g Sat); 104 mg Cholesterol; 27 g Carbohydrate; 3 g Fibre; 23 g Protein; 1285 mg Sodium

Pictured at right.

Wok? Who needs it? You can serve up some great Asian flavours right in your slow cooker. Serve this fresh-tasting delight over aromatic basmati rice.

about snow peas

Some people refer to the snow pea as mange-tout—French for "eat-all." We think it's a very fitting name indeed! Though the entire pod is edible, you may wish to remove the tough fiber that runs along the side by snapping off the stem end and pulling it down the side of the pod where the peas are attached.

Chinese Pepper Steak

Large onion, thinly sliced	1	1
Cooking oil	1 tbsp.	15 mL
Beef inside round steak, cut into strips	2 lbs.	900 g
Can of diced tomatoes (with juice)	14 oz.	398 mL
Soy sauce	1/4 cup	60 mL
Beef bouillon powder	1 tsp.	5 mL
Garlic clove, minced	1	1
(or 1/4 tsp., 1 mL, powder)		
Granulated sugar	1 tsp.	5 mL
Salt	3/4 tsp.	4 mL
Pepper	1/8 tsp.	0.5 mL
Fresh bean sprouts	1 1/2 cups	375 mL
Snow peas, trimmed	1 1/2 cups	375 mL
Medium green pepper, thinly sliced	1	1
Medium red pepper, thinly sliced	1	1
Water	3 tbsp.	50 mL
Cornstarch	2 tbsp.	30 mL

Put onion into 3 1/2 to 4 quart (3.5 to 4 L) slow cooker.

Heat large frying pan on medium-high until very hot. Add cooking oil. Add beef. Stir-fry for about 5 minutes until browned. Add to slow cooker.

Combine next 7 ingredients in medium bowl. Pour over beef. Cook, covered, on Low for 6 to 7 hours or on High for 3 to 3 1/2 hours.

Add next 4 ingredients. Stir.

Stir water into cornstarch in small cup. Add to slow cooker. Stir. Cook, covered, on High for about 15 minutes until liquid is slightly thickened and vegetables are tender-crisp. Makes about 9 cups (2.25 L).

1 cup (250 mL): 223 Calories; 8.7 g Total Fat (3.5 g Mono, 0.9 g Poly, 2.5 g Sat); 59 mg Cholesterol; 12 g Carbohydrate; 2 g Fibre; 24 g Protein; 844 mg Sodium

Pictured at right.

Dilly Beef Dinner

Diced peeled potato	4 cups	1 L
Thinly sliced carrot	3 cups	750 mL
Thinly sliced celery	3/4 cup	175 mL
Sliced (or chopped) onion	1 1/2 cups	375 mL
Flank (or brisket) steak, cut into 6 equal pieces	2 lbs.	900 g
Can of diced tomatoes (with juice)	14 oz.	398 mL
Dried dillweed	1 1/2 tsp.	7 mL
Salt	1 tsp.	5 mL
Pepper	1/4 tsp.	1 mL

Serve this dill-luxe blend of steak and veggies to your family, then sit back and watch their dill-lighted reactions.

Layer first 4 ingredients, in order given, in 5 to 7 quart (5 to 7 L) slow cooker.

Arrange steak over onion.

Combine remaining 4 ingredients in small bowl. Pour over steak. Cook, covered, on Low for 8 to 10 hours or on High for 4 to 5 hours. Serves 6.

1 serving: 415 Calories; 13.7 g Total Fat (5.5 g Mono, 0.6 g Poly, 5.7 g Sat); 64 mg Cholesterol; 33 g Carbohydrate; 5 g Fibre; 38 g Protein; 725 mg Sodium

Chinese Pepper Steak, page 52

Don't be fooled by the name. The curry spice in this hotpot is actually quite mild. Sweet, fruity and nice, it's best served over rice.

food fun

When you bite into an apricot, whether fresh or dried, consider that apricots were once believed to cause fever. Foolish superstition? Perhaps, but one with a grain of truth to it—or should we say, a seed? If digested the seed inside the apricot releases a type of cyanide that can, indeed, make you sick if eaten in large amounts. But stick to the delicious fruit and you can't go wrong.

Beef Curry Hotpot

Cooking oil	1 tbsp.	15 mL
Beef inside round (or blade) steak, trimmed of fat and cut into 1 inch (2.5 cm) cubes	2 lbs.	900 g
Medium cooking apples (such as McIntosh), peeled and chopped	3	3
Medium onions, sliced	2	2
Chopped tomato	2 cups	500 mL
Curry powder	2 tsp.	10 mL
Can of condensed beef broth	10 oz.	284 mL
Water	1 cup	250 mL
Chopped dried apricot	1/2 cup	125 mL
Raisins	1/3 cup	75 mL
All-purpose flour	1 tbsp.	15 mL
Brown sugar, packed	1 tbsp.	15 mL
Pepper, sprinkle		

Heat cooking oil in large frying pan on medium-high. Add beef. Cook for 5 to 10 minutes, stirring occasionally, until no longer pink. Transfer to 4 to 5 quart (4 to 5 L) slow cooker.

Add apple and onion to same frying pan. Cook on medium for about 5 minutes, stirring often, until softened. Add to slow cooker.

Add tomato and curry powder to same frying pan. Heat and stir for about 2 minutes until heated through. Add to slow cooker.

Add next 4 ingredients. Stir. Cook, covered, on Low for 6 to 8 hours or on High for 3 to 4 hours.

Combine remaining 3 ingredients in small cup. Add to slow cooker. Stir. Cook, covered, on High for 10 to 15 minutes until boiling and slightly thickened. Makes about 8 cups (2 L).

1 cup (250 mL): 272 Calories; 8.2 g Total Fat (3.3 g Mono, 0.9 g Poly, 2.3 g Sat); 67 mg Cholesterol; 24 g Carbohydrate; 3 g Fibre; 26 g Protein; 343 mg Sodium

Hungarian Goulash

Chopped onion	1 1/2 cups	375 mL
All-purpose flour	2 tbsp.	30 mL
Paprika	2 tsp.	10 mL
Garlic powder	1/4 tsp.	1 mL
Salt	1 tsp.	5 mL
Pepper	1/4 tsp.	1 mL
Stewing beef, cut into 3/4 inch (2 cm) cubes	1 1/2 lbs.	680 g
Can of diced tomatoes (with juice)	14 oz.	398 mL
Beef bouillon powder	2 tsp.	10 mL
Granulated sugar	1 tsp.	5 mL
Liquid gravy browner (optional)	1/2 tsp.	2 mL
Sour cream	1/2 cup	125 mL

This hearty beef and tomato blend gets its distinctive flavour from a healthy portion of paprika and just enough sour cream to give it a touch of tang. Superb!

Put onion into 3 1/2 to 4 quart (3.5 to 4 L) slow cooker.

Combine next 5 ingredients in large resealable freezer bag. Add beef. Seal bag. Toss until coated. Add to slow cooker. Discard any remaining flour mixture.

Combine next 4 ingredients in medium bowl. Add to slow cooker. Stir. Cook, covered, on Low for 8 to 10 hours or on High for 4 to 5 hours.

Add sour cream. Stir. Serves 6.

1 serving: 273 Calories; 13.4 g Total Fat (5.2 g Mono, 0.6 g Poly, 6.2 g Sat); 71 mg Cholesterol; 11 g Carbohydrate; 1 g Fibre; 27 g Protein; 1004 mg Sodium

Comfort food goes exotic. Ginger, garlic, sherry and Asian vegetables turn a humble stew into a Far East feast. Serve over rice noodles.

tip

To slice meat easily, place it in the freezer for about 30 minutes until it's just starting to freeze, and then cut. If using from frozen state, partially thaw before cutting.

Ginger Beef Stew

Medium onions, cut into wedges	2	2
Medium carrot, sliced diagonally	1	1
Can of sliced water chestnuts, drained	8 oz.	227 mL
Roasted red peppers, drained and blotted dry, cut into strips	1 cup	250 mL
Cooking oil	1 tbsp.	15 mL
Beef inside round steak, trimmed of fat and cut into 1/2 inch (12 mm) thick slices	1 1/2 lbs.	680 g
Finely grated gingerroot (or 1 1/2 tsp., 7 mL, ground ginger)	2 tbsp.	30 mL
Garlic cloves, minced (or 1/2 tsp., 2 mL, powder)	2	2
Water	2/3 cup	150 mL
Dry sherry (or prepared beef broth)	1/4 cup	60 mL
Brown sugar, packed	1 tbsp.	15 mL
Soy sauce	3 tbsp.	50 mL
Cornstarch	1 tbsp.	15 mL
Snow peas, trimmed	1 cup	250 mL

Layer first 4 ingredients, in order given, in 3 1/2 quart (3.5 L) slow cooker.

Heat cooking oil in large frying pan on medium. Add beef. Cook for 8 to 10 minutes, stirring occasionally, until browned.

Add ginger and garlic. Heat and stir for about 1 minute until fragrant.

Add next 3 ingredients. Stir. Bring to a boil. Pour over red pepper. Cook, covered, on Low for 8 to 9 hours or on High for 4 to 4 1/2 hours.

Stir soy sauce into cornstarch in small cup. Add to slow cooker. Stir. Add snow peas. Stir. Cook, covered, on High for about 10 minutes until snow peas are tender-crisp and sauce is boiling and thickened. Makes about 5 cups (1.25 L).

1 cup (250 mL): 335 Calories; 11.6 g Total Fat (4.8 g Mono, 1.3 g Poly, 3.2 g Sat); 80 mg Cholesterol; 23 g Carbohydrate; 5 g Fibre; 32 g Protein; 739 mg Sodium

Pictured at right.

Get all your wining and dining done with one fantastic and rather fancy-tasting dish. Great served with noodles or mashed potatoes.

about slow cooker safety

Slow cookers heat foods at a relatively low temperature that is still hot enough to safely prevent bacteria from growing—but don't assume there are no safety issues involved with slow cookers. Never let your ingredients warm to room temperature before turning the slow cooker on. If you want to do the preparation the night before, keep the ingredients separate and refrigerated until it is time to turn the slow cooker on. And if you have a slow cooker with a timer, make sure the timer is set for no longer than two hours after you've left the food in it. Finally, never, never use a slow cooker to reheat food.

Beef In Red Wine

All-purpose flour	3 tbsp.	50 mL
Salt, sprinkle		
Stewing beef, cut into 1 1/2 inch (3.8 cm) cubes	1 lb.	454 g
Cooking oil	2 tsp.	10 mL
Thinly sliced onion	2 cups	500 mL
Thinly sliced carrot	1 cup	250 mL
Dry (or alcohol-free) red wine	1 cup	250 mL
Garlic cloves, minced (or 1/2 tsp., 2 mL, powder)	2	2
Pepper	1/4 tsp.	1 mL
Bay leaves	2	2
Sprig of fresh rosemary (or thyme)	1	1

Combine flour and salt in large resealable freezer bag. Add beef. Seal bag. Toss until coated.

Heat cooking oil in large frying pan on medium-high. Add beef. Discard any remaining flour mixture. Cook for about 5 minutes, stirring occasionally, until browned. Transfer to 3 1/2 quart (3.5 L) slow cooker.

Layer onion and carrot, in order given, over beef.

Combine next 3 ingredients in small bowl. Pour over carrot. Add bay leaves and rosemary sprig. Cook, covered, on Low for 6 to 8 hours or on High for 3 to 4 hours. Discard bay leaves and rosemary sprig. Makes about 4 cups (1 L).

1 cup (250 mL): 429 Calories; 16.2 g Total Fat (7.4 g Mono, 1.5 g Poly, 5.5 g Sat); 84 mg Cholesterol; 20 g Carbohydrate; 3 g Fibre; 35 g Protein; 125 mg Sodium

Pictured at right.

Onion Beef Ragout

Stewing beef, cut into 3/4 inch (2 cm) cubes	2 lbs.	900 g
Envelope of green peppercorn sauce mix	1 1/4 oz.	38 g
Medium onions, cut into 8 wedges each	3	3
Water	1 cup	250 mL
Dry (or alcohol-free) red wine	1/2 cup	125 mL

Put beef into 4 to 5 quart (4 to 5 L) slow cooker. Sprinkle with sauce mix. Stir until coated. Arrange onion over beef.

Combine water and wine in small bowl. Pour over onion. Cook, covered, on Low for 8 to 9 hours or on High for 4 to 4 1/2 hours. Makes about 8 cups (2 L).

1 cup (250 mL): 237 Calories; 10.2 g Total Fat (4.2 g Mono, 0.4 g Poly, 4.0 g Sat); 63 mg Cholesterol; 8 g Carbohydrate; 1 g Fibre; 26 g Protein; 349 mg Sodium

Pictured below.

Let's call it stew—French-style. So easy and tasty the French would have only one word for it: magnifique! Serve with mashed potatoes and green beans.

Top: Beef In Red Wine, page 58
Bottom: Onion Beef Ragout, above

"Steak" out your claim to great taste with this hearty medley of beef and veggies in a tomato sauce.

money-saving tip

Think of your slow cooker as your penny-pinching friend. You can use less-tender, inexpensive cuts of meat and they'll become tender and succulent with slow cooking. Buy these cuts in bulk, freeze and use in your slow cooker.

Steak Bake

Medium onion, sliced	1	1
Medium peeled potatoes, quartered	4	4
Medium carrots, sliced	4	4
Beef inside round (or blade) steak, cut into 6 equal pieces	2 lbs.	900 g
Can of diced tomatoes (with juice)	14 oz.	398 mL
Can of condensed tomato soup	10 oz.	284 mL
Salt	1 tsp.	5 mL
Pepper	1/4 tsp.	1 mL
Garlic powder	1/4 tsp.	1 mL
Water	1/4 cup	60 mL
All-purpose flour	2 tbsp.	30 mL
Can of cut green beans, drained	14 oz.	398 mL
Chopped green onion, for garnish		

Layer first 4 ingredients, in order given, in 5 to 7 quart (5 to 7 L) slow cooker.

Combine next 5 ingredients in medium bowl. Pour over steak. Cook, covered, on Low for 8 to 10 hours or on High for 4 to 5 hours. Transfer steak to plate using slotted spoon. Cover to keep warm.

Stir water into flour in small cup until smooth. Add to slow cooker. Stir. Cook, covered, on High for 15 minutes until boiling and slightly thickened.

Add green beans and steak. Stir until heated through.

Garnish with green onion. Serves 6.

1 serving: 381 Calories; 11.2 g Total Fat (4.0 g Mono, 0.9 g Poly, 3.6 g Sat); 88 mg Cholesterol; 36 g Carbohydrate; 4 g Fibre; 37 g Protein; 1163 mg Sodium

Pictured at right.

Take it slow with this rich and decadent classic. Tender beef in a creamy red wine tomato sauce just shouldn't be rushed. Serve over egg noodles or rice.

tip

If a recipe calls for less than an entire can of tomato paste, freeze the unopened can for 30 minutes. Open both ends and push the contents through one end. Slice off only what you need and freeze the remaining paste in a resealable freezer bag or plastic wrap for future use.

Slow Stroganoff Stew

Ingredient	Imperial	Metric
All-purpose flour	3 tbsp.	50 mL
Stewing beef	2 lbs.	900 g
Cooking oil	2 tbsp.	30 mL
Cooking oil	2 tsp.	10 mL
Sliced fresh white mushrooms	1 1/2 cups	375 mL
Thinly sliced onion	1 1/2 cups	375 mL
Paprika	2 tsp.	10 mL
Can of diced tomatoes (with juice)	14 oz.	398 mL
Dry (or alcohol-free) red wine	1/2 cup	125 mL
Prepared beef broth	1/2 cup	125 mL
Tomato paste (see Tip)	3 tbsp.	50 mL
Granulated sugar	1/2 tsp.	2 mL
Salt	1/4 tsp.	1 mL
Pepper	1/4 tsp.	1 mL
Sour cream	1/3 cup	75 mL

Measure flour into large resealable freezer bag. Add beef. Seal bag. Toss until coated.

Heat first amount of cooking oil in large frying pan on medium. Add beef. Discard any remaining flour. Cook for 8 to 10 minutes, stirring occasionally, until browned. Transfer to 3 1/2 to 4 quart (3.5 to 4 L) slow cooker.

Heat second amount of cooking oil in same frying pan on medium. Add mushrooms and onion. Cook for 5 to 10 minutes, stirring occasionally and scraping any brown bits from bottom of pan, until onion is softened.

Add paprika. Heat and stir for 1 minute. Add to slow cooker.

Add next 7 ingredients. Stir. Cook, covered, on Low for 9 to 10 hours or on High for 4 1/2 to 5 hours.

Add sour cream. Stir. Makes about 5 1/2 cups (1.4 L).

1 cup (250 mL): 446 Calories; 23.6 g Total Fat (10.7 g Mono, 2.7 g Poly, 7.8 g Sat); 97 mg Cholesterol; 16 g Carbohydrate; 1 g Fibre; 38 g Protein; 527 mg Sodium

Sauerkraut Beef Dinner

Chopped onion	1 cup	250 mL
Jar of sauerkraut, rinsed and well drained	28 oz.	796 mL
Beef inside round steak, trimmed of fat and cut into 1 inch (2.5 cm) cubes	2 lbs.	900 g
Can of diced tomatoes (with juice)	14 oz.	398 mL
Prepared beef broth	1/4 cup	60 mL
Tomato paste (see Tip, page 62)	2 tbsp.	30 mL
Caraway seed	1 tsp.	5 mL
Garlic clove, minced (or 1/4 tsp., 1 mL, powder)	1	1
Granulated sugar	1 tsp.	5 mL
Salt	1/4 tsp.	1 mL
Pepper	1/2 tsp.	2 mL
Red potatoes, halved lengthwise and cut into 1/4 inch (6 mm) slices	1 lb.	454 g

Layer first 3 ingredients, in order given, in 4 to 5 quart (4 to 5 L) slow cooker.

Combine next 8 ingredients in medium bowl. Pour over beef.

Arrange potato over top. Cook, covered, on Low for 8 to 10 hours or on High for 4 to 5 hours. Transfer potato to plate using slotted spoon. Transfer beef and sauerkraut mixture to serving bowl using slotted spoon. Discard any remaining liquid in slow cooker. Serves 8.

1 serving: 255 Calories; 8.1 g Total Fat (2.9 g Mono, 0.5 g Poly, 2.7 g Sat); 66 mg Cholesterol; 19 g Carbohydrate; 4 g Fibre; 26 g Protein; 971 mg Sodium

Aromatic caraway seed adds an unexpected anise-like flavour to tangy sauerkraut, tender beef and juicy tomatoes. Complete with red potatoes, it's a full meal deal.

about caraway seeds

Caraway seeds have been recommended as a cure-all for everything from colds to tooth decay, but caraway is most prized for its aromatically delicate licorice taste with its sharp underlying bite. If you're a fan of this savoury seed, lightly toast it and add it to stews, sauerkraut and soups for a nifty new taste sensation.

Here's another one of our most-requested slow cooker recipes. Readers and staff enjoy these fajitas because of the combination of tender spiced beef and both soft-cooked and crisp vegetables.

Slow Cooker Fajitas

Beef sirloin tip steak, cut into thin strips, about 3 inches (7.5 cm) long	1 1/2 lbs.	680 g
Thickly sliced fresh white mushrooms	2 cups	500 mL
Large onion, cut into 8 wedges	1	1
Medium red pepper, cut into 1/2 inch (12 mm) wide strips	1	1
Medium yellow pepper, cut into 1/2 inch (12 mm) wide strips	1	1
Finely chopped pickled jalapeño pepper (see Tip), optional	1 tbsp.	15 mL
Water	1/4 cup	60 mL
Envelope of fajita seasoning mix	1 oz.	28 g
Flour tortillas (7 1/2 inch, 19 cm, diameter)	10	10
Ripe medium avocado, diced	1	1
Lemon juice	2 tsp.	10 mL
Shredded lettuce, lightly packed	1 cup	250 mL
Grated jalapeño Monterey Jack cheese	2/3 cup	150 mL
Light (or fat-free) sour cream	2/3 cup	150 mL
Medium tomato, seeds removed and diced	1	1

Put first 6 ingredients into 3 1/2 to 4 quart (3.5 to 4 L) slow cooker.

Stir water into seasoning mix in small bowl until smooth. Add to slow cooker. Stir. Cook, covered, on Low for 5 to 6 hours or on High for 2 1/2 to 3 hours.

Drain liquid from slow cooker into medium bowl (see Note). Makes about 5 cups (1.25 L) beef mixture. Spoon beef mixture down centre of each tortilla.

Toss avocado and lemon juice in small bowl. Spoon over beef mixture on each tortilla.

Layer remaining 4 ingredients over avocado on each tortilla. Fold bottom ends of tortillas over filling. Fold in sides, slightly overlapping, leaving top ends open. Makes 10 fajitas.

1 fajita: 428 Calories; 17.7 g Total Fat (5.0 g Mono, 1.4 g Poly, 5.7 g Sat); 40 mg Cholesterol; 46 g Carbohydrate; 3 g Fibre; 22 g Protein; 819 mg Sodium

Pictured at right.

Note: The remaining liquid can be frozen and used for soup or to replace broth in another recipe.

A rich chili you can easily customize to your own heat preference. Mild as is, but you can add more chili powder to boost the fire factor.

Chili

Cooking oil	2 tsp.	10 mL
Lean ground beef	1 lb.	454 g
Chopped onion	1 cup	250 mL
Green pepper, chopped	1	1
Can of red kidney beans (with liquid)	14 oz.	398 mL
Can of condensed tomato soup	10 oz.	284 mL
Can of sliced mushrooms, drained	10 oz.	284 mL
Chili powder	1 tsp.	5 mL
Granulated sugar	1 tsp.	5 mL
Seasoned salt	1/4 tsp.	1 mL
Salt	1/2 tsp.	2 mL
Pepper	1/8 tsp.	0.5 mL

Heat cooking oil in large frying pan on medium. Add beef. Scramble-fry for about 10 minutes until no longer pink. Drain.

Layer onion and green pepper, in order given, in 3 1/2 to 4 quart (3.5 to 4 L) slow cooker.

Combine remaining 8 ingredients in medium bowl. Add beef. Stir. Pour over green pepper. Cook, covered, on Low for 6 to 7 hours or on High for 3 to 3 1/2 hours. Makes about 5 1/2 cups (1.4 L).

1 cup (250 mL): 286 Calories; 9.5 g Total Fat (3.9 g Mono, 1.2 g Poly, 2.9 g Sat); 45 mg Cholesterol; 26 g Carbohydrate; 7 g Fibre; 24 g Protein; 984 mg Sodium

Forget the tidy beef patty, and get downright sloppy with this saucy topping. Add some slices of cucumber and tomato, and serve on open-faced, toasted hamburger buns.

Beefy Bun Topping

Cooking oil	2 tsp.	10 mL
Lean ground beef	2 lbs.	900 g
Large onion, chopped	1	1
Can of diced tomatoes (with juice)	14 oz.	398 mL
Can of tomato paste	5 1/2 oz.	156 mL
Brown sugar, packed	1 1/2 tbsp.	25 mL
Chili powder	1 tbsp.	15 mL
Beef bouillon powder	2 tsp.	10 mL
Dry mustard	1/2 tsp.	2 mL
Pepper	1/4 tsp.	1 mL

(continued on next page)

Heat cooking oil in large frying pan on medium. Add beef. Scramble-fry for about 10 minutes until no longer pink. Drain.

Put onion into 3 1/2 to 4 quart (3.5 to 4 L) slow cooker. Add beef.

Combine remaining 7 ingredients in medium bowl. Add to slow cooker. Stir. Cook, covered, on Low for 5 to 6 hours or on High for 2 1/2 to 3 hours. Makes about 6 cups (1.5 L).

1/2 cup (125 mL): 158 Calories; 6.8 g Total Fat (3.0 g Mono, 0.5 g Poly, 2.5 g Sat); 42 mg Cholesterol; 7 g Carbohydrate; 1 g Fibre; 17 g Protein; 356 mg Sodium

Pictured below.   Beefy Bun Topping, page 66

Lasagna without the layering. Once again our readers have spoken and voted this recipe one of their all-time slow cooker favourites.

about garnishes

The slow cooking process often drains foods of their vibrant colours, so to add a dash of panache to your finished recipes, consider garnishing your slow cooker masterpieces with sprinkles of vibrant fresh veggies like chopped green onion and diced tomato, or give fresh herbs a try.

Lasagna

Water	12 cups	3 L
Salt	1 1/2 tsp	7 mL
Lasagna noodles, broken up	8	8
Cooking oil	2 tsp.	10 mL
Lean ground beef	1 1/2 lbs.	680 g
Cans of diced tomatoes (with juice), 14 oz. (398 mL) each	2	2
Grated mozzarella cheese	2 cups	500 mL
2% cottage cheese	1 cup	250 mL
Finely chopped onion	3/4 cup	175 mL
Can of tomato paste	5 1/2 oz.	156 mL
Granulated sugar	2 tsp.	10 mL
Parsley flakes	1 tsp.	5 mL
Dried oregano	1/2 tsp.	2 mL
Salt	1 1/4 tsp.	6 mL
Pepper	1/2 tsp.	2 mL
Dried basil	1/4 tsp.	1 mL
Garlic powder	1/4 tsp.	1 mL

Combine water and salt in Dutch oven. Bring to a boil. Add noodles. Boil, uncovered, for 12 to 14 minutes, stirring occasionally, until tender but firm. Drain.

Heat cooking oil in large frying pan on medium. Add beef. Scramble-fry for about 10 minutes until no longer pink. Drain. Transfer to 3 1/2 to 4 quart (3.5 to 4 L) slow cooker.

Add remaining 12 ingredients. Stir. Add noodles. Stir. Cook, covered, on Low for 7 to 9 hours or on High for 3 1/2 to 4 1/2 hours. Makes about 10 cups (2.5 L).

1 cup (250 mL): 320 Calories; 12.0 g Total Fat (4.4 g Mono, 0.7 g Poly, 5.7 g Sat); 58 mg Cholesterol; 27 g Carbohydrate; 2 g Fibre; 26 g Protein; 747 mg Sodium

Bolognese Sauce

Olive (or cooking) oil	2 tsp.	10 mL
Chopped pancetta (or regular bacon)	4 oz.	113 g
Lean ground beef	2 lbs.	900 g
Finely chopped carrot	2 cups	500 mL
Finely chopped celery	2 cups	500 mL
Finely chopped onion	1 1/2 cups	375 mL
Cans of tomato sauce (14 oz., 398 mL, each)	2	2
Prepared beef broth	2 cups	500 mL
Dry (or alcohol-free) white wine	1 cup	250 mL
Can of evaporated milk	5 1/2 oz.	160 mL

Heat olive oil in large frying pan on medium. Add bacon. Cook for about 4 minutes, stirring occasionally, until almost crisp. Increase heat to medium-high.

Add next 4 ingredients. Scramble-fry for about 10 minutes until beef is no longer pink. Drain. Transfer to 4 to 5 quart (4 to 5 L) slow cooker.

Add next 3 ingredients. Stir. Cook, covered, on Low for 6 to 8 hours or on High for 3 to 4 hours. Skim and discard fat from surface of liquid in slow cooker.

Add evaporated milk. Stir. Cook, covered, on High for about 10 minutes until heated through. Makes about 10 2/3 cups (2.7 L).

1 cup (250 mL): 237 Calories; 9.8 g Total Fat (4.9 g Mono, 0.8 g Poly, 4.3 g Sat); 52 mg Cholesterol; 13 g Carbohydrate; 2 g Fibre; 21 g Protein; 808 mg Sodium

We've put a glamorous twist on Bolognese by adding pancetta, white wine and evaporated milk to make a decadently creamy mixture.

about pancetta

Pancetta (pronounced pan-CHEH-tuh) is an Italian variety of bacon that has been cured with spices but not smoked like most other types of bacon. It is usually rolled into a sausage-like shape, and when sliced is patterned with swirls. It will keep in the fridge for up to three weeks and in the freezer for up to six months.

This perennial potluck pleaser also makes a great kid-pleasing entree when served over rice.

"Sweetish" Meatballs

Box of frozen cooked meatballs	2 1/4 lbs.	1 kg
Salt, sprinkle		
Pepper, sprinkle		
Can of condensed tomato soup	10 oz.	284 mL
Brown sugar, packed	3/4 cup	175 mL
White vinegar	1/2 cup	125 mL

Put meatballs into 4 to 5 quart (4 to 5 L) slow cooker. Sprinkle with salt and pepper.

Combine remaining 3 ingredients in medium bowl. Add to slow cooker. Stir until coated. Cook, covered, on Low for 5 to 6 hours or on High for 2 1/2 to 3 hours. Serves 8.

1 serving: 411 Calories; 20.6 g Total Fat (0.1 g Mono, 0.3 g Poly, 8.3 g Sat); 55 mg Cholesterol; 32 g Carbohydrate; trace Fibre; 24 g Protein; 1006 mg Sodium

Ground beef? Steak? Too much work. Ready-made meatballs are the ultimate stew-starting time saver—perfect in this creamy dill-flavoured, chock-full-of-veggies dinner delight.

Meatball Stew

Chopped onion	1 1/2 cups	375 mL
Baby carrots	3 1/2 cups	875 mL
Baby potatoes, larger ones cut in half	2 lbs.	900 g
Dried dillweed	1 1/2 tsp.	7 mL
Pepper	1/2 tsp.	2 mL
Box of frozen cooked meatballs	2 1/4 lbs.	1 kg
Can of condensed cream of mushroom soup	10 oz.	284 mL
Prepared beef broth	1 cup	250 mL
Water	1/2 cup	125 mL
Worcestershire sauce	2 tsp.	10 mL
Frozen peas	1 1/2 cups	375 mL

Layer first 3 ingredients, in order given, in 5 to 7 quart (5 to 7 L) slow cooker.

Sprinkle with dill and pepper. Arrange meatballs over top.

Combine next 4 ingredients in medium bowl. Pour over meatballs. Cook, covered, on Low for 8 to 10 hours or on High for 4 to 5 hours.

(continued on next page)

Add peas. Stir. Cook, covered, on High for about 5 minutes until heated through. Serves 8.

1 serving: 506 Calories; 22.8 g Total Fat (0.1 g Mono, 0.3 g Poly, 8.8 g Sat); 56 mg Cholesterol; 45 g Carbohydrate; 5 g Fibre; 29 g Protein; 1288 mg Sodium

Pictured below.   Meatball Stew, page 70

Sounds fancy, tastes like it too, but it's easy to prepare this delicious French stew! Coq is chicken, vin is wine—supper's ready—come, let's dine!

about cleaning mushrooms

Are you one of those people who actually peel their mushrooms? Stop wasting your time! Mushrooms are actually quite delicate and all they need is a gentle brushing to get them suitably clean. Only wash your mushrooms just before using them. You can use a special mushroom brush to gently remove any dirt and then quickly rinse under water to avoid waterlogging. Don't have a mushroom brush? A soft-bristled toothbrush works just as well.

Coq Au Vin

Bacon slices, diced	6	6
All-purpose flour	1/4 cup	60 mL
Paprika	1/4 tsp.	1 mL
Boneless, skinless chicken thighs (about 3 oz., 85 g, each)	12	12
Halved fresh white mushrooms	4 cups	1 L
Chopped onion	1 cup	250 mL
Garlic clove, minced (or 1/4 tsp., 1 mL, powder)	1	1
Can of condensed cream of mushroom soup	10 oz.	284 mL
Dry (or alcohol-free) red wine	1/2 cup	125 mL
Prepared chicken broth	1/2 cup	125 mL
Bay leaves	2	2
Dried thyme	1/2 tsp.	2 mL

Chopped fresh parsley, for garnish

Cook bacon in large frying pan on medium until crisp. Transfer with slotted spoon to paper towel-lined plate to drain. Set aside.

Heat 1 tbsp. (15 mL) drippings in same frying pan on medium. Combine flour and paprika in large resealable freezer bag. Add half of chicken. Seal bag. Toss until coated. Repeat with remaining chicken. Discard any remaining flour mixture. Add chicken to frying pan in 2 batches. Cook for 8 to 10 minutes per batch, turning occasionally, until browned. Transfer to 3 1/2 to 4 quart (3.5 to 4 L) slow cooker.

Add next 3 ingredients to same frying pan. Cook for about 2 minutes, scraping any brown bits from bottom of pan, until onion starts to soften.

Add next 5 ingredients and bacon. Heat and stir for about 2 minutes until mixture just starts to boil. Pour over chicken. Cook, covered, on Low for 7 to 8 hours or on High for 3 1/2 to 4 hours. Discard bay leaves. Transfer chicken mixture to serving platter.

Garnish with parsley. Serves 6.

1 serving: 361 Calories; 18.2 g Total Fat (6.3 g Mono, 3.1 g Poly, 5.2 g Sat); 108 mg Cholesterol; 13 g Carbohydrate; 1 g Fibre; 31 g Protein; 694 mg Sodium

Pictured at right and on back cover.

These succulent drumsticks are cooked in a deep, rich gravy that's great served over mashed potatoes.

Drumstick Bake

Chicken drumsticks, skin removed (3 – 5 oz., 85 – 140 g, each), see Note	12	12
Can of condensed cream of chicken soup	10 oz.	284 mL
Onion flakes	2 tbsp.	30 mL
Liquid gravy browner (optional)	1/2 tsp.	2 mL

Arrange drumsticks in 3 1/2 to 4 quart (3.5 to 4 L) slow cooker.

Combine remaining 3 ingredients in small bowl. Pour over chicken. Cook, covered, on Low for 6 to 7 hours or on High for 3 to 3 1/2 hours. Serves 6.

1 serving: 200 Calories; 7.0 g Total Fat (1.3 g Mono, 1.1 g Poly, 1.9 g Sat); 99 mg Cholesterol; 6 g Carbohydrate; trace Fibre; 27 g Protein; 446 mg Sodium

Note: When removing skin from drumsticks, grasp it with a paper towel. This will give a good grip on the otherwise slippery skin.

This tomato-based chicken and vegetable sauce is easy to prepare and always a great favourite. Serve over spaghetti and add crusty rolls on the side.

Chicken Cacciatore

Chopped onion	1 1/2 cups	375 mL
Chopped celery	1 1/2 cups	375 mL
Chopped green pepper	1 1/2 cups	375 mL
Boneless, skinless chicken breast halves, halved	1 lb.	454 g
Boneless, skinless chicken thighs	1 lb.	454 g
Can of crushed tomatoes	14 oz.	398 mL
Can of stewed tomatoes, chopped (see Note)	14 oz.	398 mL
Garlic cloves, minced (or 1/2 tsp., 2 mL, powder)	2	2
Dried oregano	1 1/2 tsp.	7 mL
Bay leaf	1	1
Dried basil	1 tsp.	5 mL
Dried rosemary, crushed	1/2 tsp.	2 mL
Granulated sugar	1/2 tsp.	2 mL
Salt	1/2 tsp.	2 mL
Pepper	1/4 tsp.	1 mL

(continued on next page)

Layer first 5 ingredients, in order given, in 4 to 5 quart (4 to 5 L) slow cooker.

Combine next 10 ingredients in medium bowl. Pour over chicken. Cook, covered, on Low for 8 to 10 hours or on High for 4 to 5 hours. Discard bay leaf. Serves 8.

1 serving: 202 Calories; 6.3 g Total Fat (2.3 g Mono, 1.5 g Poly, 1.7 g Sat); 70 mg Cholesterol; 12 g Carbohydrate; 2 g Fibre; 24 g Protein; 407 mg Sodium

Pictured below.

Note: Cut tomatoes with a paring knife or kitchen shears while still in the can.

Chicken Cacciatore, page 74

Got a ragin' Cajun hunger? With a pot of this hearty sausage and chicken stew, Mardi Gras is just a slow cooker away. Serve over rice.

food fun

Creole and Cajun food are two types of cuisine popular in Louisiana. Although they share some of the same ingredients, their origins are quite different. Creole and Cajun are not just types of cuisine, they also represent cultural heritage. A person who is Creole has a multi-racial heritage with African and Caribbean roots. A person who claims Cajun ancestry has ties to the French Acadians who originally settled in modern-day Nova Scotia and moved south. Although both groups relocated to Southern Louisiana, their origins are very different and their cooking is influenced by their original heritage and the local foodstuffs available in Louisiana.

Cajun Chicken

Cooking oil	2 tbsp.	30 mL
Chopped onion	1 1/2 cups	375 mL
Chopped red pepper	1 cup	250 mL
Chopped celery	1/3 cup	75 mL
Garlic cloves, minced (or 1 tsp., 5 mL, powder)	4	4
All-purpose flour	2 tbsp.	30 mL
Sliced green onion	1/3 cup	75 mL
Lean kielbasa (or smoked ham) sausage ring, cut into 6 pieces and halved lengthwise	10 oz.	285 g
Boneless, skinless chicken thighs (about 3 oz., 85 g, each)	10	10
Bay leaf	1	1
Can of condensed chicken broth	10 oz.	284 mL
Chili sauce	1/2 cup	125 mL
Chili powder	1 1/2 tsp.	7 mL
Dried basil	1/2 tsp.	2 mL
Dried oregano	1/2 tsp.	2 mL
Ground thyme	1/4 tsp.	1 mL
Pepper	1/4 tsp.	1 mL

Heat cooking oil in large frying pan on medium-high. Add next 4 ingredients. Cook for 3 to 4 minutes, stirring often, until onion is softened.

Sprinkle with flour. Heat and stir for 1 minute. Transfer to 4 to 5 quart (4 to 5 L) slow cooker.

Layer next 3 ingredients, in order given, over vegetable mixture. Add bay leaf.

Combine next 7 ingredients in same frying pan. Heat and stir on medium for 5 minutes, scraping any brown bits from bottom of pan. Pour over chicken. Cook, covered, on Low for 7 to 8 hours or on High for 3 1/2 to 4 hours. Serves 8.

1 serving: 275 Calories; 13.8 g Total Fat (4.7 g Mono, 2.7 g Poly, 2.3 g Sat); 63 mg Cholesterol; 13 g Carbohydrate; 1 g Fibre; 24 g Protein; 1106 mg Sodium

Pictured at right.

Roll out the slow cooker, and we'll have a slow cooker of fun! OK, our polka may not be up to snuff, but these ham and chicken rolls, covered in Swiss cheese, are sure to put the oompahpah into your dinner.

about swiss cheese

Ever wondered what gives Swiss cheese its characteristic holes or "eyes?" During the fermentation process carbon dioxide is released which creates the bubbles that later form the holes in the cheese. The Swiss cheese we are familiar with in North America is quite mild tasting because it is only aged for about four months. The real Swiss cheeses that hail from the land of neutrality, Emmenthal and Gruyère, although similar in colour, are aged longer and have a stronger flavour. All three cheeses melt well and are great in fondues.

Stuffed Chicken Rolls

Boneless, skinless chicken breast halves (4 – 6 oz., 113 – 170 g, each)	6	6
Thin deli ham slices (about 4 oz., 113 g)	6	6
Dry (or alcohol-free) white wine	1/2 cup	125 mL
Hot water	1/2 cup	125 mL
Chicken bouillon powder	2 tsp.	10 mL
Dried marjoram	1/2 tsp.	2 mL
Salt	1/2 tsp.	2 mL
Pepper	1/4 tsp.	1 mL
Liquid gravy browner (optional)	1 tsp.	5 mL
Grated Swiss cheese	1 cup	250 mL
Water	2 1/2 tbsp.	37 mL
Cornstarch	1 tbsp.	15 mL

Place chicken breasts between 2 sheets of plastic wrap. Pound with mallet or rolling pin to 1/2 inch (12 mm) thickness. Place 1 ham slice on each chicken breast. Roll up tightly, jelly roll-style. Secure with wooden picks. Arrange in 3 1/2 to 4 quart (3.5 to 4 L) slow cooker.

Combine next 7 ingredients in small bowl. Pour over rolls. Cook, covered, on Low for 8 to 9 hours or on High for 4 to 4 1/2 hours. Transfer rolls to serving dish using slotted spoon.

Sprinkle cheese over rolls. Cover to keep warm.

Stir water into cornstarch in small cup. Add to slow cooker. Stir. Cook, covered, on High for about 15 minutes until boiling and slightly thickened. Serve with rolls. Serves 6.

1 serving: 414 Calories; 10.0 g Total Fat (1.1 g Mono, 1.0 g Poly, 4.5 g Sat); 182 mg Cholesterol; 3 g Carbohydrate; trace Fibre; 69 g Protein; 1057 mg Sodium

Pictured at right.

Chicken And Stuffing Meal

Baby carrots, sliced lengthwise	1/2 lb.	225 g
Baby potatoes, larger ones cut in half	1 lb.	454 g
Boneless, skinless chicken breast halves, cut into bite-sized pieces	1 1/2 lbs.	680 g
Can of condensed cream of chicken soup	10 oz.	284 mL
Frozen peas	2 cups	500 mL
Hot water	1/2 cup	125 mL
Butter (or hard margarine)	2 tbsp.	30 mL
Box of stove-top stuffing mix	4 1/4 oz.	120 g

Layer first 3 ingredients, in order given, in 3 1/2 to 4 quart (3.5 to 4 L) slow cooker.

Whisk soup in small bowl until smooth. Add peas. Stir. Spoon over chicken.

Stir hot water and butter in medium heatproof bowl until butter is melted. Add stuffing mix and seasoning packet. Stir. Spoon over chicken mixture. Cook, covered, on Low for 8 to 9 hours or on High for 4 to 4 1/2 hours. Serves 6.

1 serving: 407 Calories; 10.9 g Total Fat (1.5 g Mono, 0.7 g Poly, 3.7 g Sat); 80 mg Cholesterol; 41 g Carbohydrate; 5 g Fibre; 34 g Protein; 828 mg Sodium

Tender chicken and veggies with a creamy stuffing—the perfect Sunday night fare (made all the more perfect by its easy preparation).

tip

It is important to clean the cutting board and any utensils used to cut raw chicken or any other meat in hot, soapy water. This will prevent bacteria from spreading to other food.

Stuffed Chicken Rolls, page 78

Strike up the band with these delicious savoury drumettes. Serve with fries on the side and call it a dinner well played.

Parmesan Chicken Drumettes

Plain yogurt	3/4 cup	175 mL
Chicken drumettes (or split chicken wings, tips discarded)	3 lbs.	1.4 kg
Grated Parmesan cheese	1 1/2 cups	375 mL
Fine dry bread crumbs	1/3 cup	75 mL
Paprika	1 1/2 tsp.	7 mL
Parsley flakes	1 1/2 tsp.	7 mL
Seasoned salt	1 1/2 tsp.	7 mL

Measure yogurt into extra-large bowl. Add chicken. Stir until coated.

Combine remaining 5 ingredients in large resealable freezer bag. Add 1/3 of chicken. Seal bag. Toss until coated. Repeat with remaining chicken. Put chicken into greased 3 1/2 to 4 quart (3.5 to 4 L) slow cooker. Discard any remaining yogurt and cheese mixture. Cook, covered, on Low for 8 to 9 hours or on High for 4 to 4 1/2 hours. Transfer chicken with slotted spoon to serving platter. Discard any remaining liquid in slow cooker. Makes about 24 drumettes (or 36 wing pieces).

1 drumette: 159 Calories; 10.9 g Total Fat (3.7 g Mono, 2 g Poly, 3.5 g Sat); 48 mg Cholesterol; 1 g Carbohydrate; trace Fibre; 13 g Protein; 210 mg Sodium

Pictured at right.

A sure bet is that peanut butter will up the ante in this saucy chicken dish. Serve it over noodles, rice or couscous, and all the peanut lovers will cash in—big time!

about zucchini

Although a zucchini's outward appearance resembles a cucumber, the first is actually a squash, and the latter is a gourd. Zucchini's flowers, when cooked, are considered quite a delicacy. The zucchini is a favourite of gardeners because it does well in temperate climates and can grow to almost monstrous proportions—sometimes nearing three feet in length! However, outside the county fair, smaller zucchinis are preferable because they are more tender and less fibrous than larger ones. When storing zucchini, keep it in the crisper so it doesn't get too soft. And because zucchini has a high water content, it is not advisable to freeze it.

Peanut Butter Chicken

Ingredient	Imperial	Metric
Olive (or cooking) oil	2 tsp.	10 mL
Medium onions, sliced	2	2
Garlic cloves, minced (or 1/2 tsp., 2 mL, powder)	2	2
Baby carrots	2 cups	500 mL
Bone-in chicken parts, skin removed (see Note)	3 1/2 lbs.	1.6 kg
Can of tomato sauce	7 1/2 oz.	213 mL
Brown sugar, packed	1 tbsp.	15 mL
Curry powder	1 tsp.	5 mL
Peanut butter	1/2 cup	125 mL
Plain yogurt (not non-fat)	1/2 cup	125 mL
Olive (or cooking) oil	2 tsp.	10 mL
Medium zucchini (with peel), quartered lengthwise and cut crosswise into 3/4 inch (2 cm) slices	2	2
Coarsely chopped unsalted peanuts (optional)	2 tbsp.	30 mL

(Handwritten annotations: "Cook in slow cooker 1-8", "L or 3.5-4", "H - 3.5-4 HRS", "then Add")

Heat first amount of olive oil in large frying pan on medium. Add onion and garlic. Cook for about 10 minutes, stirring often, until onion is softened and starting to brown. Transfer to 3 1/2 to 4 quart (3.5 to 4 L) slow cooker.

Layer carrots and chicken, in order given, over onion mixture.

Combine next 3 ingredients in small bowl. Pour over chicken. Cook, covered, on Low for 7 to 8 hours or on High for 3 1/2 to 4 hours. Transfer chicken to serving dish using slotted spoon. Cover to keep warm.

Combine peanut butter and yogurt in small bowl. Add to slow cooker. Stir. Cook, covered, on Low for about 5 minutes until heated through.

Heat second amount of olive oil in large frying pan on medium-high. Add zucchini. Cook for about 5 minutes, stirring often, until starting to brown. Add to slow cooker. Stir. Pour over chicken.

Sprinkle with peanuts. Serves 6.

(continued on next page)

1 serving: 644 Calories; 32.6 g Total Fat (13.0 g Mono, 7.7 g Poly, 7.7 g Sat); 170 mg Cholesterol; 23 g Carbohydrate; 4 g Fibre; 65 g Protein; 474 mg Sodium

Pictured below.

Note: Use whichever cuts of chicken you prefer as long as the weight used is equal to that listed.

Mama mia! A proper parmigiana in a slow cooker? Sì, certo (yes, of course)! This dish is simple to prepare and simply superb to dine on.

Chicken Parmigiana

Medium eggplant (with peel), cut into 3/4 inch (2 cm) slices	1	1
Boneless, skinless chicken breast halves (4 – 6 oz., 113 – 170 g, each)	6	6
Cans of pizza sauce (7 1/2 oz., 213 mL, each)	2	2
Salt	1 tsp.	5 mL
Pepper	1/4 tsp.	1 mL
Grated part-skim mozzarella cheese	1 1/2 cups	375 mL
Grated Parmesan cheese	1 tbsp.	15 mL

Layer eggplant and chicken, in order given, in 5 to 7 quart (5 to 7 L) slow cooker.

Combine next 3 ingredients in small bowl. Pour over chicken. Cook, covered, on Low for 6 to 7 hours or on High for 3 to 3 1/2 hours.

Sprinkle with mozzarella and Parmesan cheese. Cook, covered, on High for about 5 minutes until cheese is melted. Serves 6.

1 serving: 552 Calories; 17.3 g Total Fat (5.6 g Mono, 4.1 g Poly, 5.2 g Sat); 159 mg Cholesterol; 12 g Carbohydrate; 5 g Fibre; 79 g Protein; 1140 mg Sodium

Pictured at right.

Rah, rah raspberry! Three cheers for this MVI (most valuable ingredient). Sweet yet tangy, all the stats agree— this dish is a sure winner! (Remember to allow plenty of time for the chicken to properly marinate.)

Raspberry Chicken

Raspberry jam	1 cup	250 mL
Dry (or alcohol-free) white wine	2/3 cup	150 mL
Raspberry red wine vinegar	1/2 cup	125 mL
Soy sauce	2 tbsp.	30 mL
Dijon mustard	2 tsp.	10 mL
Garlic cloves, minced (or 1/2 tsp., 2 mL, powder)	2	2
Chicken legs, back attached (11 – 12 oz., 310 – 340 g, each), skin removed	8	8
Water	1/4 cup	60 mL
Cornstarch	2 tbsp.	30 mL
Chopped fresh parsley, for garnish		

(continued on next page)

Combine first 6 ingredients in small bowl. Transfer to large resealable freezer bag.

Add chicken. Turn until coated. Let stand, covered, in refrigerator for at least 4 hours or overnight, turning occasionally. Transfer chicken with raspberry mixture to 4 to 5 quart (4 to 5 L) slow cooker. Cook, covered, on Low for 8 to 9 hours or on High for 4 to 4 1/2 hours. Transfer chicken to serving dish using slotted spoon. Skim and discard fat from surface of liquid in slow cooker.

Stir water into cornstarch in small cup. Add to slow cooker. Stir. Cook, covered, on High for about 5 minutes until boiling and thickened. Pour over chicken.

Garnish with parsley. Serves 8.

1 serving: 265 Calories; 3.4 g Total Fat (1.1 g Mono, 0.9 g Poly, 0.9 g Sat); 108 mg Cholesterol; 29 g Carbohydrate; trace Fibre; 26 g Protein; 334 mg Sodium

Pictured below.

Top: Raspberry Chicken, page 84
Bottom: Chicken Parmigiana, page 84

Slow-simmered with a hint of smokiness from the bacon and a touch of tanginess from the sour cream, this tender chicken dish could be considered a delicious embarrassment of riches. Serve over potatoes or pasta.

Rich Chicken Stew

Bacon slices, diced	2	2
Medium onion, sliced	1	1
Chopped fresh white mushrooms	1 cup	250 mL
All-purpose flour	2 tbsp.	30 mL
Diced carrot	1 1/2 cups	375 mL
Diced celery (with leaves)	1 1/2 cups	375 mL
Bone-in chicken parts, skin removed (see Note)	3 lbs.	1.4 kg
Can of condensed chicken broth	10 oz.	284 mL
Parsley flakes	1 tbsp.	15 mL
Dried sage	1/2 tsp.	2 mL
Dried thyme	1/2 tsp.	2 mL
Salt	1/4 tsp.	1 mL
Pepper	1/4 tsp.	1 mL
Sour cream	2/3 cup	150 mL
All-purpose flour	2 tbsp.	30 mL

Cook bacon in large frying pan on medium-high until crisp. Add onion and mushrooms. Cook for 3 to 4 minutes, stirring often, until onion starts to brown.

Sprinkle with first amount of flour. Heat and stir for 1 minute. Transfer to 4 to 5 quart (4 to 5 L) slow cooker.

Layer next 3 ingredients, in order given, over mushroom mixture.

Combine next 6 ingredients in same frying pan. Heat and stir on medium for 5 minutes, scraping any brown bits from bottom of pan. Pour over chicken. Cook, covered, on Low for 7 to 8 hours or on High for 3 1/2 to 4 hours. Transfer chicken to serving dish using slotted spoon. Cover to keep warm.

Stir sour cream into second amount of flour in small bowl until smooth. Add to slow cooker. Stir. Cook, covered, on High for about 5 minutes until slightly thickened. Pour over chicken. Serves 6.

1 serving: 405 Calories; 15.5 g Total Fat (5.8 g Mono, 2.6 g Poly, 6.6 g Sat); 177 mg Cholesterol; 12 g Carbohydrate; 2 g Fibre; 52 g Protein; 685 mg Sodium

Note: Use whichever cuts of chicken you prefer as long as the weight used is equal to that listed.

Orange Chicken

Hot water	1/4 cup	60 mL
Chicken bouillon powder	1 tsp.	5 mL
Reserved mandarin orange juice		
Orange juice	1 cup	250 mL
Finely chopped fresh rosemary	2 tsp.	10 mL
(or 1/2 tsp., 2 mL, dried, crushed)		
Lemon pepper	1 tsp.	5 mL
Paprika	1/2 tsp.	2 mL
Salt (optional)	1/4 tsp.	1 mL
Bone-in chicken parts, skin removed	3 lbs.	1.4 kg
(see Note)		
Water	2 tbsp.	30 mL
Cornstarch	2 tbsp.	30 mL
Can of mandarin orange segments,	10 oz.	284 mL
drained and juice reserved		

Chopped fresh rosemary, for garnish

A guaranteed hit with the kids, this dish has no onions or green bits, but plenty of sweet orange pieces. Even adults will love the succulent citrus flavour. Serve over rice.

Stir hot water into bouillon powder in small bowl until dissolved. Add mandarin orange juice.

Add next 5 ingredients. Stir. Transfer to 3 1/2 quart (3.5 L) slow cooker.

Add chicken, pressing into juice mixture. Cook, covered, on Low for 7 to 8 hours or on High for 3 1/2 to 4 hours.

Stir water into cornstarch in small bowl. Add to slow cooker. Stir. Cook, covered, on High for about 15 minutes until boiling and thickened.

Add orange segments. Stir gently.

Garnish with rosemary. Serves 4.

1 serving: 477 Calories; 10.8 g Total Fat (3.1 g Mono, 2.6 g Poly, 2.7 g Sat); 238 mg Cholesterol; 17 g Carbohydrate; 1 g Fibre; 74 g Protein; 637 mg Sodium

Pictured on page 89.

Note: Use whichever cuts of chicken you prefer as long as the weight used is equal to that listed.

Cardamom and cinnamon unite with a variety of spices to produce a spicy, yet subtly sweet taste reminiscent of many Moroccan dishes. Serve over rice or couscous.

tip

To bruise cardamom, pound pods with mallet or press with flat side of a wide knife to "bruise," or crack them open slightly.

tip

When toasting nuts, seeds or coconut, cooking times will vary for each type of nut—so never toast them together. For small amounts, place ingredient in an ungreased shallow frying pan. Heat on medium for 3 to 5 minutes, stirring often, until golden. For larger amounts, spread ingredient evenly in an ungreased shallow pan. Bake in a 350°F (175°C) oven for 5 to 10 minutes, stirring or shaking often, until golden.

Moroccan Chicken

Cooking oil	2 tsp.	10 mL
Thinly sliced onion	2 cups	500 mL
Garlic cloves, minced	2	2
(or 1/2 tsp., 2 mL, powder)		
Finely grated gingerroot	1/2 tsp.	2 mL
Chili powder	1/2 tsp.	2 mL
Ground coriander	1/2 tsp.	2 mL
Ground cumin	1/2 tsp.	2 mL
Boneless, skinless chicken thighs, halved	1 lb.	454 g
Dry white wine (or prepared chicken broth)	1/2 cup	125 mL
Liquid honey	2 tbsp.	30 mL
Cinnamon stick (4 inches, 10 cm)	1	1
Whole green cardamom, bruised	6	6
(see Tip), or 1/4 tsp. (1 mL) ground		
Salt, sprinkle		
Orange juice	1/4 cup	60 mL
Cornstarch	2 tsp.	10 mL
Slivered almonds, toasted	3 tbsp.	50 mL
(see Tip), optional		

Heat cooking oil in large frying pan on medium. Add next 3 ingredients. Cook for 5 to 10 minutes, stirring often, until onion is softened and starting to brown.

Add next 3 ingredients. Heat and stir for 1 to 2 minutes until fragrant. Transfer to 3 1/2 quart (3.5 L) slow cooker.

Add next 6 ingredients. Stir. Cook, covered, on Low for 7 to 8 hours or on High for 3 1/2 to 4 hours.

Stir orange juice into cornstarch in small bowl. Add to slow cooker. Stir. Cook, covered, on High for about 15 minutes until boiling and thickened. Remove and discard cinnamon stick and cardamom pods.

Sprinkle with almonds. Serves 4.

1 serving: 288 Calories; 11.0 g Total Fat (4.6 g Mono, 2.7 g Poly, 2.6 g Sat); 74 mg Cholesterol; 20 g Carbohydrate; 1 g Fibre; 21 g Protein; 77 mg Sodium

Pictured at right.

Top: Orange Chicken, page 87
Bottom: Moroccan Chicken, above

Free up some time in your evening—make dinner in the morning instead! This delicious sauce cooks while you're out and about. Put some pasta on when you get home and dinner's on the table in minutes!

Mushroom Chicken Sauce

Bacon slices, diced	6	6
Cooking oil	1 tbsp.	15 mL
Chopped onion	1 cup	250 mL
Sliced fresh white mushrooms	3 cups	750 mL
Garlic cloves, minced (or 1/2 tsp., 2 mL, powder)	2	2
Paprika	1 tsp.	5 mL
All-purpose flour	3 tbsp.	50 mL
Salt	1/4 tsp.	1 mL
Pepper	1/4 tsp.	1 mL
Boneless, skinless chicken thighs, cut into 3/4 inch (2 cm) cubes	1 1/2 lbs.	680 g
Dry (or alcohol-free) white wine	1/2 cup	125 mL
Prepared chicken broth	1/2 cup	125 mL
Frozen peas	1/2 cup	125 mL
Chopped fresh parsley (or 1 tbsp., 15 mL, flakes)	1/4 cup	60 mL
Sour cream	1/4 cup	60 mL

Cook bacon in large frying pan on medium for about 5 minutes until almost crisp. Transfer with slotted spoon to paper towel-lined plate to drain. Drain and discard drippings from pan.

Heat cooking oil in same frying pan on medium. Add onion. Cook for 5 to 10 minutes, stirring often, until softened.

Add next 3 ingredients. Cook for about 5 minutes, stirring occasionally, until mushrooms are softened. Add bacon. Stir. Spread evenly in 3 1/2 quart (3.5 L) slow cooker.

Combine next 3 ingredients in large resealable freezer bag. Add chicken. Seal bag. Toss until coated. Arrange chicken over mushroom mixture. Discard any remaining flour mixture.

Pour wine and broth over chicken. Cook, covered, on Low for 8 to 9 hours or on High for 4 to 4 1/2 hours.

(continued on next page)

Add remaining 3 ingredients. Stir. Cook, covered, on High for about 10 minutes until heated through. Makes about 5 1/4 cups (1.3 L).

1 cup (250 mL): 333 Calories; 17.7 g Total Fat (7.2 g Mono, 3.5 g Poly, 5.2 g Sat); 98 mg Cholesterol; 10 g Carbohydrate; 1 g Fibre; 29 g Protein; 526 mg Sodium

Curious Chicken Chili

Cooking oil	2 tsp.	10 mL
Boneless, skinless chicken thighs, cut into 1/2 inch (12 mm) pieces	1 lb.	454 g
Chopped onion	1 1/2 cups	375 mL
Chopped green pepper	1 cup	250 mL
Diced jalapeño pepper (see Tip)	1 tbsp.	15 mL
Garlic cloves, minced (or 1/2 tsp., 2 mL, powder)	2	2
Salt	1 tsp.	5 mL
Can of diced tomatoes (with juice)	14 oz.	398 mL
Can of pineapple chunks (with juice)	14 oz.	398 mL
Can of red kidney beans, rinsed and drained	14 oz.	398 mL
Hot (or cold) strong prepared coffee	1 cup	250 mL
Can of diced green chilies	4 oz.	113 g
Tomato paste (see Tip)	3 tbsp.	50 mL
Chili powder	2 tbsp.	30 mL
Semi-sweet chocolate baking square (1 oz., 28 g), grated	1	1
Ground cumin	1 tsp.	5 mL

Heat cooking oil in large frying pan on medium-high. Add chicken. Cook for about 5 minutes, stirring often, until browned.

Add next 5 ingredients. Cook for about 5 minutes, stirring often, until onion starts to soften. Transfer to 3 1/2 to 4 quart (3.5 to 4 L) slow cooker.

Add remaining 9 ingredients. Stir. Cook, covered, on Low for 4 hours or on High for 2 hours. Makes about 8 cups (2 L).

1 cup (250 mL): 349 Calories; 7.5 g Total Fat (2.4 g Mono, 1.8 g Poly, 2.1 g Sat); 37 mg Cholesterol; 50 g Carbohydrate; 10 g Fibre; 23 g Protein; 516 mg Sodium

Pictured on page 93.

Curious as to why this chili is such a curiosity? It's all in the ingredients— coffee, chocolate, jalapeño and pineapple. This is a chili you just have to taste. Go ahead, we know you want to.

tip

If a recipe calls for less than an entire can of tomato paste, freeze the unopened can for 30 minutes. Open both ends and push the contents through one end. Slice off only what you need and freeze the remaining paste in a resealable freezer bag or plastic wrap for future use.

tip

Hot peppers contain capsaicin in the seeds and ribs. If you like less spice in your food, removing the seeds and ribs will reduce the heat. Wear rubber gloves when handling hot peppers and avoid touching your eyes—and always wash your hands well afterwards.

Get ready to wow the crowd with these beautiful bright red peppers stuffed with black beans, corn, chicken and couscous.

tip

Don't be tempted to lift the lid on your slow cooker and give the contents a stir unless a recipe specifically asks you to do so. The lid actually becomes vacuum sealed by the heat and steam. If you lift the lid, the steam will escape, which can add 15 to 20 minutes onto your cooking time. As for stirring? It isn't always necessary because your slow cooker heats from the sides, not from the bottom, to keep the cooking even.

Corn And Bean-Stuffed Peppers

Large red peppers	6	6
Long grain white (or brown) rice	1/4 cup	60 mL
Cooking oil	1 tsp.	5 mL
Lean ground chicken	3/4 lb.	340 g
Canned black beans, rinsed and drained	1 cup	250 mL
Frozen kernel corn	1 cup	250 mL
Sliced green onion	1/4 cup	60 mL
Garlic clove, minced (or 1/4 tsp., 1 mL, powder), optional	1	1
Seasoned salt	1/2 tsp.	2 mL
Dried basil	1/4 tsp.	1 mL
Dried oregano	1/4 tsp.	1 mL
Pepper	1/4 tsp.	1 mL
Can of diced tomatoes (with juice)	14 oz.	398 mL
Couscous, approximately	2/3 cup	150 mL
Chopped fresh parsley (or cilantro), for garnish		

Trim 1/4 inch (6 mm) slice from top of each red pepper. Remove and discard seeds and ribs. Sprinkle 2 tsp. (10 mL) rice into each red pepper. Place red peppers upright in 5 to 7 quart (5 to 7 L) slow cooker.

Heat cooking oil in large frying pan on medium-high. Add chicken. Scramble-fry for about 5 minutes until no longer pink. Remove from heat.

Add next 8 ingredients. Stir. Spoon into red peppers.

Pour tomatoes with juice over red peppers. Cook, covered, on Low for 5 hours or on High for 2 1/2 hours. Transfer red peppers to serving dish. Cover to keep warm.

Pour liquid from slow cooker into 2 cup (500 mL) liquid measure. Add equal amount of couscous to liquid. Stir. Let stand, covered, for about 5 minutes until liquid is absorbed. Spoon couscous into red peppers.

Garnish with parsley. Serves 6.

1 serving: 312 Calories; 8.4 g Total Fat (trace Mono, 0.3 g Poly, 0.1 g Sat); 0 mg Cholesterol; 45 g Carbohydrate; 7 g Fibre; 17 g Protein; 512 mg Sodium

Pictured at right.

Top: Corn And Bean-Stuffed Peppers, page 92
Bottom: Curious Chicken Chili, page 91

Got a hankerin' for some good old southwestern sandwich flavour? Then, yee doggies, this is the meal for you! Sweet and tangy with an authentic taste.

Pulled Tex Turkey

Sliced onion	1 1/2 cups	375 mL
Barbecue sauce	1 cup	250 mL
Can of tomato sauce	7 1/2 oz.	213 mL
Can of diced green chilies	4 oz.	113 g
Chili powder	1 tbsp.	15 mL
Dried oregano	1 tsp.	5 mL
Ground cumin	1/2 tsp.	2 mL
Ground cinnamon	1/4 tsp.	1 mL
Boneless, skinless turkey thighs	1 3/4 lbs.	790 g
Kaiser rolls, split (toasted, optional)	6	6

Combine first 8 ingredients in 3 1/2 to 4 quart (3.5 to 4 L) slow cooker. Add turkey. Spoon barbecue sauce mixture over turkey to cover. Cook, covered, on Low for 7 to 8 hours or on High for 3 1/2 to 4 hours. Remove turkey to cutting board using tongs. Shred turkey using 2 forks. Add to sauce mixture. Stir. Makes about 4 cups (1 L) turkey mixture.

Serve turkey mixture in rolls. Makes 6 sandwiches.

1 sandwich: 534 Calories; 22.5 g Total Fat (1.0 g Mono, 1.4 g Poly, 6.9 g Sat); 126 mg Cholesterol; 44 g Carbohydrate; 5 g Fibre; 39 g Protein; 981 mg Sodium

We're not full of beans but this delicious, mildly curry-flavoured delight has four kinds of them—and some peaches for good measure!

Full-Of-Beans Turkey Pot

Cans of sliced peaches in light syrup (with syrup), 14 oz. (398 mL) each	2	2
Boneless, skinless turkey thighs, cut into 1 inch (2.5 cm) pieces	1 1/2 lbs.	680 g
Can of black beans, rinsed and drained	19 oz.	540 mL
Can of red kidney beans, rinsed and drained	19 oz.	540 mL
Can of white kidney beans, rinsed and drained	19 oz.	540 mL
Can of baked beans in tomato sauce	14 oz.	398 mL
Chopped green pepper	1 cup	250 mL
Chopped onion	1 cup	250 mL
Sweet (or regular) chili sauce	1/2 cup	125 mL
Curry powder	1 tsp.	5 mL

(continued on next page)

Combine all 10 ingredients in 4 to 5 quart (4 to 5 L) slow cooker. Cook, covered, on Low for 8 to 10 hours or on High for 4 to 5 hours. Makes about 12 cups (3 L).

1 cup (250 mL): 329 Calories; 8.9 g Total Fat (trace Mono, trace Poly, 2.7 g Sat); 54 mg Cholesterol; 43 g Carbohydrate; 11 g Fibre; 22 g Protein; 678 mg Sodium

Pictured below.

Full-Of-Beans Turkey Pot, page 94

Take turkey back from the holidays and start making it weekday fare. This turkey roast cooks up juicy and tender in the slow cooker. And the leftovers make amazing sandwiches.

about cleaning slow cookers

Keeping your cooker clean is always very important. Any missed debris may become baked on the next time you use it and can be almost impossible to remove. Some slow cookers come with removable liners that can be popped directly into the sink or dishwasher. Or you can line your slow cooker with a heatproof plastic cooking bag for speedy cleanups when pressed for time. And need we say it? Never submerge the electric components of your slow cooker!

Turkey Roast Supreme

Baby carrots	2 cups	500 mL
Sliced celery	1 2/3 cups	400 mL
Olive (or cooking) oil	1 tbsp.	15 mL
Sliced onion	1 1/2 cups	375 mL
Garlic cloves, minced (or 1/2 tsp., 2 mL, powder)	2	2
Olive (or cooking) oil	1 tsp.	5 mL
Paprika	1 tsp.	5 mL
Pepper	1 tsp.	5 mL
Turkey breast roast	2 1/2 lbs.	1.1 kg
Prepared chicken broth	1 cup	250 mL
Italian no-salt seasoning	2 tsp.	10 mL
Evaporated milk	3/4 cup	175 mL
All-purpose flour	2 tbsp.	30 mL

Layer carrots and celery, in order given, in 3 1/2 to 4 quart (3.5 to 4 L) slow cooker.

Heat first amount of olive oil in large frying pan on medium. Add onion. Cook for about 10 minutes, stirring often, until onion is softened and starting to brown. Add to slow cooker.

Combine next 4 ingredients in small dish.

Rub spice mixture on roast. Place over onion in slow cooker.

Pour broth around roast. Sprinkle with seasoning. Cook, covered, on Low for 7 to 8 hours or on High for 3 1/2 to 4 hours. Transfer roast to cutting board. Cover with foil. Let stand for 10 minutes.

Stir evaporated milk into flour in small bowl until smooth. Add to slow cooker. Stir. Cook, covered, on High for about 15 minutes until boiling and slightly thickened. Cut roast into thin slices. Arrange on serving platter. Spoon vegetables and sauce over top. Serves 8.

1 serving: 249 Calories; 4.2 g Total Fat (2.1 g Mono, 0.7 g Poly, 1.0 g Sat); 90 mg Cholesterol; 13 g Carbohydrate; 2 g Fibre; 38 g Protein; 323 mg Sodium

Pictured at right.

You don't need meat for a rich hearty stew. The firm, meaty texture of eggplant acts as a satisfying meat replacement in this veggie-laden dish.

Ratatouille

Sliced zucchini (with peel), 1/4 inch (6 mm) thick	3 cups	750 mL
Small eggplant (with peel), cut into 1/2 inch (12 mm) cubes	1	1
Can of diced tomatoes (with juice)	14 oz.	398 mL
Chopped celery	1 cup	250 mL
Finely chopped onion	1 cup	250 mL
Medium green (or red) pepper, chopped	1	1
Ketchup	1/4 cup	60 mL
Granulated sugar	2 tsp.	10 mL
Parsley flakes	1 tsp.	5 mL
Dried basil	1/2 tsp.	2 mL
Dried oregano	1/2 tsp.	2 mL
Garlic powder	1/4 tsp.	1 mL
Salt	1/2 tsp.	2 mL
Pepper	1/8 tsp.	0.5 mL

Combine all 14 ingredients in 3 1/2 to 4 quart (3.5 to 4 L) slow cooker. Cook, covered, on Low for 8 to 9 hours or on High for 4 to 4 1/2 hours. Makes about 6 1/2 cups (1.6 L).

1 cup (250 mL): 72 Calories; 0.4 g Total Fat (trace Mono, 0.2 g Poly, 0.1 g Sat); 0 mg Cholesterol; 17 g Carbohydrate; 5 g Fibre; 3 g Protein; 480 mg Sodium

Pictured on page 101.

The enticing Italian flavour in this subtly spiced, meatless stew makes it particularly pleasing—and the dumplings finish it off perfectly!

Squash And Dumplings

Cans of Italian-style stewed tomatoes (14 oz., 398 mL, each)	2	2
Can of mixed beans, rinsed and drained	19 oz.	540 mL
Small fresh whole white mushrooms, halved	2 cups	500 mL
Butternut squash, cut into 1/2 inch (12 mm) pieces	3/4 lb.	340 g
Water	1 cup	250 mL
Garlic cloves, minced (or 1/2 tsp., 2 mL, powder)	2	2
Italian seasoning	2 tsp.	10 mL
Pepper	1/4 tsp.	1 mL

(continued on next page)

DUMPLINGS

All-purpose flour	1/2 cup	125 mL
Yellow cornmeal	1/3 cup	75 mL
Grated Parmesan cheese	2 tbsp.	30 mL
Baking powder	1 tsp.	5 mL
Paprika	1/8 tsp.	0.5 mL
Large egg	1	1
Cooking oil	2 tbsp.	30 mL
Milk	2 tbsp.	30 mL
Basil pesto	1 tsp.	5 mL

Combine first 8 ingredients in 4 to 5 quart (4 to 5 L) slow cooker. Cook, covered, on Low for 8 to 9 hours or on High for 4 to 4 1/2 hours. Bring to a boil on High.

Dumplings: Measure first 5 ingredients into medium bowl. Stir. Make a well in centre.

Beat remaining 4 ingredients with fork in small bowl. Add to well. Stir until just moistened. Spoon mounds of batter, using 2 tbsp. (30 mL) for each, in single layer over squash mixture. Cook, covered, on High for 40 to 50 minutes until wooden pick inserted in centre of dumpling comes out clean. Serves 6.

1 serving: 271 Calories; 7.0 g Total Fat (3.2 g Mono, 1.7 g Poly, 1.0 g Sat); 33 mg Cholesterol; 43 g Carbohydrate; 8 g Fibre; 11 g Protein; 506 mg Sodium

Pictured below.

Squash And Dumplings, page 98

This mellow yellow dish gets its colour from curry powder and its distinctive flavour from ginger and coconut milk. The mellow part? That's you getting a little R 'n' R while it cooks!

about slow cooker cookery

Don't assume that just any recipe can go in the slow cooker. Liquids will never reach a full boil in the slow cooker and any ground meat needs to be browned before going in for safety reasons. Also, you need to consider that some vegetables will cook faster than others and may end up soggy if put in too early. To take advantage of the ease of the slow cooker, it's best to use recipes that are specially designed for them.

Vegetable Curry

Can of coconut milk	14 oz.	398 mL
All-purpose flour	1 1/2 tbsp.	25 mL
Curry powder	2 tsp.	10 mL
Cauliflower florets	3 cups	750 mL
Chopped peeled potato	3 cups	750 mL
Can of chickpeas (garbanzo beans), rinsed and drained	19 oz.	540 mL
Chopped carrot	2 cups	500 mL
Chopped onion	1 2/3 cups	400 mL
Finely grated gingerroot	1 tbsp.	15 mL
Garlic cloves, minced (or 1/2 tsp., 2 mL, powder)	2	2
Salt	1 tsp.	5 mL
Frozen peas	1/2 cup	125 mL

Whisk first 3 ingredients in small bowl until smooth.

Put next 8 ingredients in 5 to 7 quart (5 to 7 L) slow cooker. Add coconut milk mixture. Stir. Cook, covered, on Low for 7 to 8 hours or on High for 3 1/2 to 4 hours.

Add peas. Stir gently. Cook, covered, on High for about 5 minutes until heated through. Makes about 8 1/2 cups (2.1 L).

1 cup (250 mL): 258 Calories; 11.4 g Total Fat (0.7 g Mono, 0.8 g Poly, 8.9 g Sat); 0 mg Cholesterol; 35 g Carbohydrate; 8 g Fibre; 8 g Protein; 403 mg Sodium

Pictured at right.

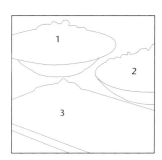

1. Ratatouille, page 98
2. Vegetable Curry, above
3. Lentil Rice Rolls, page 104

Serve this spicy bean treat with tortilla chips, salsa and sour cream on the side for your own flavour fiesta.

tip

Chipotle chili peppers are smoked jalapeño peppers so, just as with fresh jalapeños, be sure to wash your hands after handling.
To store any leftover chipotle chili peppers, divide into recipe-friendly portions and freeze, with sauce, in airtight containers for up to one year.

easy burritos

Turn Spicy Beans And Rice into super-simple burritos by spooning about 1/2 cup (125 mL) of Spicy Beans And Rice down the centre of each of 8 flour tortillas (9 inch, 22 cm, diameter). Add chopped or torn lettuce, sour cream, salsa, grated Cheddar cheese and chopped tomato. Fold in sides and roll up from the bottoms to enclose filling.

Pictured at right.

Spicy Beans And Rice

Can of red kidney beans, rinsed and drained	19 oz.	540 mL
Prepared vegetable broth	1 1/4 cups	300 mL
Chopped onion	1 cup	250 mL
Chopped red pepper	1 cup	250 mL
Chopped tomato	1 cup	250 mL
Chopped celery	1/2 cup	125 mL
Chili powder	1 tsp.	5 mL
Chopped chipotle pepper in adobo sauce (see Tip)	1 tsp.	5 mL
Dried oregano	1 tsp.	5 mL
Salt	1/2 tsp.	2 mL
Pepper	1/4 tsp.	1 mL
Converted white rice	1/2 cup	125 mL
Chopped green onion	1/3 cup	75 mL
Chopped fresh parsley (or 1 1/2 tsp., 7 mL, flakes)	2 tbsp.	30 mL
Lime juice	1 tbsp.	15 mL

Combine first 11 ingredients in 3 1/2 quart (3.5 L) slow cooker. Cook, covered, on Low for 7 to 8 hours or on High for 3 1/2 to 4 hours.

Add rice. Stir. Cook, covered, on High for about 30 minutes until rice is tender.

Add remaining 3 ingredients. Stir gently. Makes about 4 cups (1 L).

1 cup (250 mL): 238 Calories; 1.3 g Total Fat (0.1 g Mono, 0.2 g Poly, 0.1 g Sat); 0 mg Cholesterol; 46 g Carbohydrate; 15 g Fibre; 12 g Protein; 466 mg Sodium

Pictured at right.

Left: Easy Burritos, this page
Top Right: Spicy Beans And Rice, above

These ravishing roll-ups get exotic with lentils and a hint of sweetness from raisins, brown sugar and cinnamon.

tip

When a recipe calls for grated lemon zest and juice, it's easier to grate the lemon first, then juice it. Be careful not to grate down to the pith (the white part of the peel), which is bitter and best avoided.

Lentil Rice Rolls

Medium head of green cabbage (about 3 lbs., 1.4 kg)	1	1
Boiling water, to cover		
Can of lentils, rinsed and drained	19 oz.	540 mL
Can of tomato sauce	7 1/2 oz.	213 mL
Finely chopped carrot	1/2 cup	125 mL
Finely chopped celery	1/2 cup	125 mL
Finely chopped onion	1/2 cup	125 mL
Long grain brown (or white) rice	1/2 cup	125 mL
Garlic clove, minced (or 1/4 tsp., 1 mL, powder)	1	1
Dried oregano	1/2 tsp.	2 mL
Can of tomato sauce	25 oz.	680 mL
Raisins	1/4 cup	60 mL
Lemon juice	3 tbsp.	50 mL
Brown sugar, packed	2 tbsp.	30 mL
Grated lemon zest (see Tip)	2 tsp.	10 mL
Ground cinnamon	1/2 tsp.	2 mL

Remove core from cabbage. Trim about 1/2 inch (12 mm) slice from bottom. Place, cut-side down, in Dutch oven or large pot. Cover with boiling water. Cover Dutch oven with foil. Let stand for 5 minutes. Drain. Let stand until cool enough to handle. Carefully remove 10 large outer leaves from cabbage. Cut 'V' shape along tough ribs of leaves to remove. Discard ribs. Set leaves aside. Shred remaining cabbage. Put into 5 to 7 quart (5 to 7 L) slow cooker.

Combine next 8 ingredients in large bowl. Place about 1/3 cup (75 mL) lentil mixture on centre of 1 cabbage leaf. Fold in sides. Roll up tightly from bottom to enclose filling. Repeat with remaining lentil mixture and cabbage leaves.

Combine remaining 6 ingredients in medium bowl. Add 1 1/2 cups (375 mL) to slow cooker. Stir. Spread evenly. Arrange rolls, seam-side down, over top. Pour remaining tomato sauce mixture over rolls. Cook, covered, on Low for 8 to 10 hours or on High for 4 to 5 hours. Carefully transfer rolls to plate. Transfer cabbage mixture to large serving platter. Arrange rolls over top. Makes 10 rolls.

1 roll: 176 Calories; 0.5 g Total Fat (0.1 g Mono, 0.2 g Poly, 0.1 g Sat); 0 mg Cholesterol; 37 g Carbohydrate; 9 g Fibre; 7 g Protein; 664 mg Sodium

Pictured on page 101.

Chili Black Beans

Cans of black beans (19 oz., 540 mL, each), rinsed and drained	2	2
Chopped butternut squash	2 cups	500 mL
Can of diced tomatoes (with juice)	14 oz.	398 mL
Chopped onion	1 1/2 cups	375 mL
Prepared vegetable broth	1/2 cup	125 mL
Finely chopped fresh jalapeño pepper (with seeds), see Tip	2 tbsp.	30 mL
Chili powder	1 tbsp.	15 mL
Bay leaves	2	2
Garlic cloves, minced (or 1/2 tsp., 2 mL, powder)	2	2
Salt	1/4 tsp.	1 mL
Chopped green pepper	1 cup	250 mL

Combine first 10 ingredients in 3 1/2 to 4 quart (3.5 to 4 L) slow cooker. Cook, covered, on Low for 8 to 10 hours or on High for 4 to 5 hours.

Add green pepper. Stir gently. Cook, covered, on High for about 20 minutes until green pepper is tender-crisp. Discard bay leaves. Makes about 6 cups (1.5 L).

1 cup (250 mL): 176 Calories; 0.4 g Total Fat (0.1 g Mono, 0.2 g Poly, 0.1 g Sat); 0 mg Cholesterol; 43 g Carbohydrate; 12 g Fibre; 9 g Protein; 1070 mg Sodium

Pictured below.

Bean looking for a great vegetarian entree? Look no further—this spicy blend of beans and veggies is sure to win over even the most dedicated meat lover. Top with sour cream, salsa or green onion, if you desire.

tip

Hot peppers contain capsaicin in the seeds and ribs. If you like less spice in your food, removing the seeds and ribs will reduce the heat. Wear rubber gloves when handling hot peppers and avoid touching your eyes—and always wash your hands well afterwards.

Pork With Orange Sauce

This big-batch delight of tender pork in a sweet orange sauce makes enough for a crowd of eight.

Apricot jam, warmed	1/4 cup	60 mL
Dijon mustard (with whole seeds)	2 tbsp.	30 mL
Salt, sprinkle		
Pepper, sprinkle		
Pork sirloin (or boneless loin) roast	3 lbs.	1.4 kg
ORANGE SAUCE		
Hard margarine (or butter)	1 tsp.	5 mL
Finely chopped onion	1/4 cup	60 mL
Brandy (or 1 tsp., 5 mL, brandy extract)	3 tbsp.	50 mL
Orange juice	1 cup	250 mL
Prepared chicken broth	1 cup	250 mL
Dijon mustard (with whole seeds)	1 tbsp.	15 mL
Water	1 tbsp.	15 mL
Cornstarch	2 tsp.	10 mL

Combine first 4 ingredients in small cup.

Brush jam mixture over roast. Place in 4 to 5 quart (4 to 5 L) slow cooker. Cook, covered, on Low for 8 hours or on High for 4 hours. Transfer roast to cutting board. Cover with foil. Let stand for 10 minutes.

Orange Sauce: Melt margarine in medium saucepan on medium. Add onion. Cook for 5 to 10 minutes, stirring often, until softened and starting to brown.

Add brandy. Heat and stir for about 2 minutes until liquid is almost evaporated.

Add next 3 ingredients. Stir. Bring to a boil on medium-high. Boil, uncovered, for about 5 minutes until slightly reduced. Reduce heat to medium.

Stir water into cornstarch in small cup. Add to orange juice mixture. Heat and stir for about 5 minutes until boiling and thickened. Makes about 1 1/3 cups (325 mL) sauce. Cut roast into thin slices. Serve with Orange Sauce. Serves 8.

1 serving: 316 Calories; 11.9 g Total Fat (5.2 g Mono, 1.3 g Poly, 3.8 g Sat); 109 mg Cholesterol; 12 g Carbohydrate; trace Fibre; 36 g Protein; 396 mg Sodium

Pictured at right.

Built to feed and please a hungry crowd, these pulled pork sandwiches have a down-home barbecue flavour.

Barbecue Shredded Pork Sandwiches

Boneless pork shoulder butt roast	3 lbs.	1.4 kg
Can of tomato sauce	14 oz.	398 mL
Brown sugar, packed	1/2 cup	125 mL
Ketchup	1/2 cup	125 mL
Medium onion, chopped	1	1
Apple cider vinegar	1/3 cup	75 mL
Garlic cloves, minced (or 1 tsp., 5 mL, powder)	4	4
Worcestershire sauce	1 tbsp.	15 mL
Chili powder	2 tsp.	10 mL
Dry mustard	2 tsp.	10 mL
Salt	1 tsp.	5 mL
Pepper	1/2 tsp.	2 mL
Dried crushed chilies	1/2 tsp.	2 mL
Crusty rolls, split (toasted, optional)	12	12

Place roast in 3 1/2 to 4 quart (3.5 to 4 L) slow cooker.

Combine next 12 ingredients in medium bowl. Pour over roast. Cook, covered, on Low for 10 to 12 hours or on High for 5 to 6 hours. Transfer roast to cutting board. Cool slightly. Shred roast with 2 forks. Skim and discard fat from surface of liquid in slow cooker. Pour remaining liquid into large frying pan. Bring to a boil on medium. Boil gently, uncovered, for 12 to 15 minutes until thickened to a pasta sauce consistency. Add pork. Stir.

Serve pork mixture in rolls. Makes 12 sandwiches.

1 sandwich: 311 Calories; 6.1 g Total Fat (2.3 g Mono, 0.6 g Poly, 1.7 g Sat); 71 mg Cholesterol; 36 g Carbohydrate; 2 g Fibre; 29 g Protein; 843 mg Sodium

Pictured at right.

Cherry Pork Chops

Bone-in pork chops, trimmed of fat	6	6
Liquid gravy browner (optional)	1 tsp.	5 mL
Salt, sprinkle		
Pepper, sprinkle		
Cherry pie filling	1 cup	250 mL
Apple cider vinegar	1 1/2 tsp.	7 mL
Prepared mustard	1 tsp.	5 mL
Ground cloves, sprinkle		

Brush both sides of pork with gravy browner. Sprinkle with salt and pepper.

Combine remaining 4 ingredients in small bowl. Layer pork and cherry mixture in 5 to 7 quart (5 to 7 L) slow cooker. Cook, covered, on Low for 8 to 9 hours or on High for 4 to 4 1/2 hours. Transfer pork to serving plate. Spoon cherry mixture over top. Serves 6.

1 serving: 201 Calories; 6.0 g Total Fat (2.7 g Mono, 0.4 g Poly, 2.2 g Sat); 61 mg Cholesterol; 12 g Carbohydrate; trace Fibre; 23 g Protein; 62 mg Sodium

Pictured below.

Sweet cherry adds a delectable flavour twist to tender, savoury pork. Consider this dish a sweet surprise.

Top: Cherry Pork Chops, above
Bottom: Barbecue Shredded Pork Sandwiches, page 108

Tender pork and potatoes in a creamy celery-flavoured sauce make for a comforting home dinner. Double the amount of chicken spice to add a bit more kick.

Celery-Sauced Chops

Red baby potatoes, larger ones cut in half	2 lbs.	900 g
Salt, sprinkle		
Pepper, sprinkle		
Boneless pork loin chops, trimmed of fat	6	6
Montreal chicken spice	1/2 tsp.	2 mL
Pepper, just a pinch		
Cans of condensed cream of celery soup (10 oz., 284 mL, each)	2	2
Water (1 soup can)	10 oz.	284 mL

Put potatoes into 4 to 5 quart (4 to 5 L) slow cooker. Sprinkle with salt and pepper.

Arrange pork over potatoes. Sprinkle with chicken spice and pepper.

Combine soup and water in medium bowl. Pour over pork. Cook, covered, on Low for 8 to 10 hours or on High for 4 to 5 hours. Transfer pork and potatoes to serving platter using slotted spoon. Carefully process liquid in slow cooker with hand blender or in blender until smooth (see Safety Tip). Serve with pork and potatoes. Serves 6.

1 serving: 352 Calories; 10.6 g Total Fat (2.7 g Mono, 0.4 g Poly, 3.3 g Sat); 65 mg Cholesterol; 34 g Carbohydrate; 3 g Fibre; 27 g Protein; 760 mg Sodium

Pictured at right.

Safety Tip: Follow manufacturer's instructions for processing hot liquids.

Meaty chops slowly cooked in a sweet and savoury combination of peppery applesauce and creamy soup make for exquisite fare when served over noodles, rice or mashed potatoes.

Pork Chops Normandy

Medium peeled cooking apples (such as McIntosh), quartered	3	3
Boneless pork loin chops, trimmed of fat	6	6
Water	1 1/2 cups	375 mL
Can of condensed cream of mushroom soup	10 oz.	284 mL
Envelope of peppercorn sauce mix	1 1/4 oz.	38 g

Put apple into 4 to 5 quart (4 to 5 L) slow cooker. Arrange pork over apple.

(continued on next page)

Combine remaining 3 ingredients in medium bowl. Pour over pork. Cook, covered, on Low for 8 to 10 hours or on High for 4 to 5 hours. Transfer pork to serving platter. Carefully process liquid in slow cooker with hand blender or in blender until smooth. Serve with pork. Serves 6.

1 serving: 239 Calories; 9.3 g Total Fat (2.7 g Mono, 0.5 g Poly, 2.8 g Sat); 63 mg Cholesterol; 16 g Carbohydrate; 1 g Fibre; 24 g Protein; 755 mg Sodium

Pictured below.

Top: Pork Chops Normandy, page 110
Bottom: Celery-Sauced Chops, page 110

Guard your plate closely because sharing's out of the question when it comes to these brown sugar-glazed beauties.

Sweet-And-Sour Ribs

Brown sugar, packed	2 cups	500 mL
All-purpose flour	1/4 cup	60 mL
Water	1/3 cup	75 mL
White vinegar	1/2 cup	125 mL
Ketchup	2 tbsp.	30 mL
Soy sauce	2 tbsp.	30 mL
Garlic powder	1/4 tsp.	1 mL
Ground ginger	1/4 tsp.	1 mL
Pork side ribs, cut into 2 or 3 bone portions	3 lbs.	1.4 kg

Combine brown sugar and flour in medium saucepan. Add water. Stir. Add next 5 ingredients. Heat and stir on medium until boiling and thickened.

Layer ribs and brown sugar mixture in 5 to 7 quart (5 to 7 L) slow cooker. Cook, covered, on Low for 10 to 12 hours or on High for 5 to 6 hours. Serves 6.

1 serving: 720 Calories; 32.0 g Total Fat (14.2 g Mono, 2.9 g Poly, 11.7 g Sat); 128 mg Cholesterol; 77 g Carbohydrate; trace Fibre; 32 g Protein; 449 mg Sodium

Pictured at right.

The heavenly aroma of these effortless ribs will have your whole family clamouring for a taste. For best results, use well-trimmed ribs.

Easiest Ribs

Fancy (mild) molasses	1/3 cup	75 mL
Low-sodium soy sauce	1/3 cup	75 mL
Garlic cloves, minced (or 3/4 tsp., 4 mL, powder)	3	3
Dried crushed chilies	1/4 tsp.	1 mL
Sweet-and-sour-cut pork ribs, trimmed of fat and cut into 1 bone portions	3 1/2 lbs.	1.6 kg

Combine first 4 ingredients in 3 1/2 to 4 quart (3.5 to 4 L) slow cooker.

Add ribs. Stir until coated. Cook on Low for 7 to 8 hours or on High for 3 1/2 to 4 hours, stirring occasionally. Serves 6.

1 serving: 527 Calories; 38.8 g Total Fat (16.8 g Mono, 3.6 g Poly, 14.7 g Sat); 128 mg Cholesterol; 14 g Carbohydrate; trace Fibre; 29 g Protein; 561 mg Sodium

Pictured at right.

Left: Sweet-And-Sour Ribs, page 112
Right: Easiest Ribs, page 112

The saltiness of tender ham is perfectly complemented by a tangy citrus-flavoured sauce.

Slow Cooker Baked Ham

Cooked boneless ham (not frozen, see Note)	3 lbs.	1.4 kg
Brown sugar, packed	1/2 cup	125 mL
Frozen concentrated orange juice, thawed	2 tbsp.	30 mL
Dijon mustard (with whole seeds)	1 tbsp.	15 mL
Prepared horseradish	2 tsp.	10 mL
Water	2/3 cup	150 mL
Lemon juice	3 tbsp.	50 mL
Cornstarch	2 tbsp.	30 mL

Place ham in 3 1/2 to 4 quart (3.5 to 4 L) slow cooker.

Combine next 4 ingredients in small dish. Pour over ham. Cook, covered, on Low for 5 hours or on High for 2 1/2 hours. Transfer ham to cutting board. Cut into thin slices. Arrange on serving platter. Cover to keep warm.

Pour liquid from slow cooker into small saucepan. Add water.

Stir lemon juice into cornstarch in small cup. Slowly add to brown sugar mixture. Heat and stir on medium until boiling and thickened. Drizzle over ham slices. Serves 8.

1 serving: 363 Calories; 14.3 g Total Fat (6.8 g Mono, 1.7 g Poly, 4.7 g Sat); 99 mg Cholesterol; 18 g Carbohydrate; trace Fibre; 38 g Protein; 1696 mg Sodium

Note: A ham that's been frozen adds too much moisture, resulting in boiling instead of cooking.

Sausage And Potato Stew

Italian sausages, casing removed and cut into 1 inch (2.5 cm) slices	8	8
Chopped onion	1 cup	250 mL
Peeled sweet potatoes, cut into 3/4 inch (2 cm) cubes	1 lb.	454 g
Large peeled potato, cut into 1/2 inch (12 mm) cubes	1	1
Large carrot, chopped	1	1
Medium parsnips, chopped	2	2
Can of diced tomatoes (with juice)	28 oz.	796 mL
Prepared chicken broth	1 cup	250 mL
Granulated sugar	1/2 tsp.	2 mL
Pepper	1/4 tsp.	1 mL
Sour cream	1/4 cup	60 mL
Instant potato flakes	2 tbsp.	30 mL
Chopped fresh oregano	1 tbsp.	15 mL

Heat large frying pan on medium-high. Add sausage. Cook for about 10 minutes, turning occasionally, until browned. Transfer with slotted spoon to paper towel-lined plate to drain.

Layer next 5 ingredients, in order given, in 5 to 7 quart (5 to 7 L) slow cooker. Arrange sausage over top.

Combine next 4 ingredients in small bowl. Pour over sausage. Cook, covered, on Low for 8 to 10 hours or on High for 4 to 5 hours.

Add remaining 3 ingredients. Stir. Makes about 11 1/2 cups (2.9 L).

1 cup (250 mL): 272 Calories; 13.4 g Total Fat (6.0 g Mono, 1.7 g Poly, 4.9 g Sat); 39 mg Cholesterol; 26 g Carbohydrate; 3 g Fibre; 12 g Protein; 846 mg Sodium

Sweet potatoes, spicy sausage and tangy sour cream combine in this one-pot slow cooker feast.

With spicy sausage, tomatoes and a tender polenta topping, this crock-pot pie has all the best flavours of Italy.

about slow cooker leftovers

If you have leftovers that you want to save for the next day, remove them from your slow cooker as soon as possible and refrigerate. Because the walls of the slow cooker are so thick, food can't cool down quickly and safely enough in it.

Corny Shepherd's Pie

Cooking oil	1 tsp.	5 mL
Hot Italian sausage, casing removed and chopped	1 lb.	454 g
Lean ground pork	1 lb.	454 g
Chopped celery	1/2 cup	125 mL
Chopped onion	1/2 cup	125 mL
Cans of diced tomatoes (with juice), 14 oz. (398 mL) each	2	2
Frozen kernel corn	1 cup	250 mL
Dried oregano	1 tsp.	5 mL
TOPPING		
Water	3 cups	750 mL
Butter (or hard margarine)	1 tbsp.	15 mL
Pepper	1/4 tsp.	1 mL
Yellow cornmeal	1 cup	250 mL
Grated Parmesan cheese	1/2 cup	125 mL
Parsley flakes	2 tsp.	10 mL

Heat cooking oil in large frying pan on medium. Add next 4 ingredients. Scramble-fry for 8 to 10 minutes until sausage and pork are no longer pink. Drain. Transfer to 3 1/2 to 4 quart (3.5 to 4 L) slow cooker.

Add next 3 ingredients. Stir.

Topping: Measure water into medium saucepan. Bring to a boil. Reduce heat to low. Add butter and pepper. Stir. Slowly add cornmeal, stirring constantly, until water is absorbed. Cook for 2 to 3 minutes, stirring occasionally, until mixture is very thick.

Add cheese and parsley. Stir. Spread evenly over sausage mixture. Cook, covered, on Low for 8 to 9 hours or on High for 4 to 4 1/2 hours. Serves 8.

1 serving: 513 Calories; 33.9 g Total Fat (14.2 g Mono, 3.7 g Poly, 12.8 g Sat); 105 mg Cholesterol; 23 g Carbohydrate; 2 g Fibre; 29 g Protein; 870 mg Sodium

Pictured at right.

Don't worry, eat curry! With its mild coconut flavour and big pieces of lamb and vegetables, this delectable offering is sure to make all your troubles go away. Serve over rice or potatoes. (You'll be able to find coconut cream in the import section of larger grocery stores.)

about cauliflower

In case you were wondering, cauliflower comes by its floral name honestly—the white head is actually a mass of flower buds. When shopping for this awesome blossom, look for heads that are white rather than yellowish. If leaves are attached, they should look fresh and green. When home, remove the leaves and wrap the cauliflower in a plastic bag, and it will keep in your crisper for several days.

Slow Cooker Lamb Curry

All-purpose flour	2 tbsp.	30 mL
Seasoned salt	1 tsp.	5 mL
Cayenne pepper	1/4 tsp.	1 mL
Stewing lamb, trimmed of fat	1 lb.	454 g
Cooking oil	2 tbsp.	30 mL
Sliced carrot	1 1/2 cups	375 mL
Cauliflower florets	1 cup	250 mL
Coarsely chopped green pepper	1 cup	250 mL
Medium onion, coarsely chopped	1	1
Curry powder	1 tbsp.	15 mL
Garlic cloves, minced (or 1/2 tsp., 2 mL, powder)	2	2
Can of condensed chicken broth	10 oz.	284 mL
Reserved pineapple juice	1/4 cup	60 mL
Can of pineapple chunks, drained and juice reserved	14 oz.	398 mL
Grated solid coconut cream (half of 7 1/2 oz., 200 g, package)	2/3 cup	150 mL
Plain yogurt	1/2 cup	125 mL
All-purpose flour	2 tbsp.	30 mL
Chopped fresh cilantro (or mint), optional	2 tbsp.	30 mL

Combine first 3 ingredients in large resealable freezer bag. Add lamb. Seal bag. Toss until coated.

Heat cooking oil in large frying pan on medium-high. Add lamb. Discard any remaining flour mixture. Cook for about 5 minutes, stirring often, until browned. Transfer to 3 1/2 to 4 quart (3.5 to 4 L) slow cooker.

Add next 3 ingredients. Stir.

Add next 3 ingredients to same frying pan. Cook on medium for about 5 minutes until onion is softened.

(continued on next page)

Add broth and pineapple juice. Heat and stir for about 5 minutes, scraping any brown bits from bottom of pan, until boiling. Add to slow cooker. Stir. Cook, covered, on Low for 6 hours or on High for 3 hours.

Add pineapple and coconut cream. Stir.

Stir yogurt into second amount of flour in small bowl until smooth. Add to slow cooker. Stir. Cook, covered, on High for about 1 hour until sauce is boiling and thickened.

Sprinkle with cilantro. Makes about 6 1/2 cups (1.6 L).

1 cup (250 mL): 291 Calories; 15.0 g Total Fat (4.6 g Mono, 1.8 g Poly, 7.1 g Sat); 51 mg Cholesterol; 23 g Carbohydrate; 3 g Fibre; 18 g Protein; 527 mg Sodium

Pictured below.

Serve this hearty stew with the tanginess of sun-dried tomato and a hint of honey sweetness over mashed potatoes or couscous.

time-saving tip

To save time during the morning rush, prepare the onion mixture the night before and chill in a covered bowl. Then assemble and cook as directed in the morning. Dinner will be ready by the time you come home from work.

Sun-Dried Tomato Lamb

All-purpose flour	3 tbsp.	50 mL
Stewing lamb, trimmed of fat	2 lbs.	900 g
Prepared chicken broth	1 1/2 cups	375 mL
Medium onions, cut into 8 wedges each	2	2
Medium carrot, chopped	1	1
Sun-dried tomatoes in oil, blotted dry, chopped	1/2 cup	125 mL
Liquid honey	2 tbsp.	30 mL
Salt	1/4 tsp.	1 mL
Chopped fresh parsley	2 tbsp.	30 mL

Measure flour into large resealable freezer bag. Add half of lamb. Seal bag. Toss until coated. Repeat with remaining lamb. Transfer to 3 1/2 to 4 quart (3.5 to 4 L) slow cooker. Sprinkle with any remaining flour.

Add next 6 ingredients. Stir. Cook, covered, on Low for 8 to 10 hours or on High for 4 to 5 hours. Skim and discard fat from surface of liquid in slow cooker.

Add parsley. Stir. Makes about 6 cups (1.5 L).

1 cup (250 mL): 283 Calories; 9.6 g Total Fat (4.1 g Mono, 1.0 g Poly, 3.1 g Sat); 98 mg Cholesterol; 16 g Carbohydrate; 1 g Fibre; 32 g Protein; 600 mg Sodium

Pictured at right.

The slow-braised lamb in this warmly-spiced stew is sure to tempt and tantalize the taste buds. Serve over couscous or steamed rice and garnish with lemon zest.

about browning

It is important to brown some meats before they go into the slow cooker. Browning adds colour and seals in flavour but is also very important for safety reasons. Ground meats should never be put into a slow cooker without first being properly browned.

Moroccan Lamb Stew

Medium carrots, cut into 1 inch (2.5 cm) pieces	4	4
Cooking oil	2 tbsp.	30 mL
Stewing lamb, trimmed of fat	2 lbs.	900 g
Cooking oil	1 tbsp.	15 mL
Thinly sliced onion	2 cups	500 mL
Garlic cloves, minced (or 1 tsp., 5 mL, powder)	4	4
Ground cumin	2 tsp.	10 mL
Ground coriander	1 tsp.	5 mL
Ground ginger	1 tsp.	5 mL
Dried crushed chilies	1/2 tsp.	2 mL
Ground cinnamon	1/2 tsp.	2 mL
Dry (or alcohol-free) white wine	1/2 cup	125 mL
Orange juice	1/2 cup	125 mL
Brown sugar, packed	1 tbsp.	15 mL
Salt	1/4 tsp.	1 mL
Liquid honey	1 tbsp.	15 mL
Grated orange zest	1/2 tsp.	2 mL
Large pitted green olives, halved (optional)	12	12
Water	1 tbsp.	15 mL
Cornstarch	1 tbsp.	15 mL

Put carrot into 3 1/2 to 4 quart (3.5 to 4 L) slow cooker.

Heat first amount of cooking oil in large frying pan on medium-high. Add lamb in 2 batches. Cook for 8 to 10 minutes per batch, stirring occasionally, until browned. Spread evenly over carrot.

Heat second amount of cooking oil in same frying pan on medium. Add onion. Cook for 5 to 10 minutes, stirring often, until softened.

Add next 6 ingredients. Heat and stir for about 1 minute until fragrant. Spread evenly over lamb.

(continued on next page)

Combine next 4 ingredients in small bowl. Pour over onion mixture. Cook, covered, on Low for 8 to 10 hours or on High for 4 to 5 hours.

Add next 3 ingredients. Stir.

Stir water into cornstarch in small cup. Add to slow cooker. Stir. Cook, covered, on High for 5 to 10 minutes until boiling and slightly thickened. Makes about 5 1/2 cups (1.4 L).

1 cup (250 mL): 390 Calories; 16.6 g Total Fat (7.9 g Mono, 3.1 g Poly, 3.7 g Sat); 107 mg Cholesterol; 21 g Carbohydrate; 3 g Fibre; 35 g Protein; 250 mg Sodium

Pictured below.

Throughout this book measurements are given in Conventional and Metric measure. To compensate for differences between the two measurements due to rounding, a full metric measure is not always used. The cup used is the standard 8 fluid ounce. Temperature is given in degrees Fahrenheit and Celsius. Baking pan measurements are in inches and centimetres as well as quarts and litres. An exact metric conversion is given on this page as well as the working equivalent (Metric Standard Measure).

Pans

Conventional – Inches	Metric – Centimetres
8 × 8 inch	20 × 20 cm
9 × 9 inch	22 × 22 cm
9 × 13 inch	22 × 33 cm
10 × 15 inch	25 × 38 cm
11 × 17 inch	28 × 43 cm
8 × 2 inch round	20 × 5 cm
9 × 2 inch round	22 × 5 cm
10 × 4 1/2 inch tube	25 × 11 cm
8 × 4 × 3 inch loaf	20 × 10 × 7.5 cm
9 × 5 × 3 inch loaf	22 × 12.5 × 7.5 cm

Oven Temperatures

Fahrenheit (°F)	Celsius (°C)	Fahrenheit (°F)	Celsius (°C)
175°	80°	350°	175°
200°	95°	375°	190°
225°	110°	400°	205°
250°	120°	425°	220°
275°	140°	450°	230°
300°	150°	475°	240°
325°	160°	500°	260°

Spoons

Conventional Measure	Metric Exact Conversion Millilitre (mL)	Metric Standard Measure Millilitre (mL)
1/8 teaspoon (tsp.)	0.6 mL	0.5 mL
1/4 teaspoon (tsp.)	1.2 mL	1 mL
1/2 teaspoon (tsp.)	2.4 mL	2 mL
1 teaspoon (tsp.)	4.7 mL	5 mL
2 teaspoons (tsp.)	9.4 mL	10 mL
1 tablespoon (tbsp.)	14.2 mL	15 mL

Cups

1/4 cup (4 tbsp.)	56.8 mL	60 mL
1/3 cup (5 1/3 tbsp.)	75.6 mL	75 mL
1/2 cup (8 tbsp.)	113.7 mL	125 mL
2/3 cup (10 2/3 tbsp.)	151.2 mL	150 mL
3/4 cup (12 tbsp.)	170.5 mL	175 mL
1 cup (16 tbsp.)	227.3 mL	250 mL
4 1/2 cups	1022.9 mL	1000 mL (1 L)

Dry Measurements

Conventional Measure Ounces (oz.)	Metric Exact Conversion Grams (g)	Metric Standard Measure Grams (g)
1 oz.	28.3 g	28 g
2 oz.	56.7 g	57 g
3 oz.	85.0 g	85 g
4 oz.	113.4 g	125 g
5 oz.	141.7 g	140 g
6 oz.	170.1 g	170 g
7 oz.	198.4 g	200 g
8 oz.	226.8 g	250 g
16 oz.	453.6 g	500 g
32 oz.	907.2 g	1000 g (1 kg)

Casseroles

Canada & Britain		United States	
Standard Size Casserole	Exact Metric Measure	Standard Size Casserole	Exact Metric Measure
1 qt. (5 cups)	1.13 L	1 qt. (4 cups)	900 mL
1 1/2 qts. (7 1/2 cups)	1.69 L	1 1/2 qts. (6 cups)	1.35 L
2 qts. (10 cups)	2.25 L	2 qts. (8 cups)	1.8 L
2 1/2 qts. (12 1/2 cups)	2.81 L	2 1/2 qts. (10 cups)	2.25 L
3 qts. (15 cups)	3.38 L	3 qts. (12 cups)	2.7 L
4 qts. (20 cups)	4.5 L	4 qts. (16 cups)	3.6 L
5 qts. (25 cups)	5.63 L	5 qts. (20 cups)	4.5 L

Tip Index

Recipe Index

most loved recipe collection